Polymer Clay
Global Perspectives

Emerging Ideas and Techniques from 125 International Artists

Cynthia Tinapple

POTTER
CRAFT

Library of Congress Cataloging-in-Publication Data
Tinapple, Cynthia.
Polymer clay global perspectives : emerging ideas and techniques from
125 international artists / Cynthia Tinapple.
pages cm
Includes index.
1. Polymer clay craft. I. Title.
TT297.T56 2013
745.57'23–dc23
2012037060

ISBN 978-0-8230-8590-3
eISBN 978-0-8230-8591-0

Printed in China

Text design by Jenny Kraemer
Cover design by Jenny Kraemer
Cover photographs (front cover, top to bottom row, left to right): Cathy Barbaray, Genevieve Williamson, Christine Damm,
Iris Mishly, Sabine Spiesser, Eva Haskova, Sandra Trachsel, Christine Damm, Tanya Mayorova, Linda Ezerman, Genevieve
Williamson, Angie Wiggins, Kim Korringa, Gera Chandler, Rebecca Watkins, Genevieve Williamson, Donna Greenberg,
Lisa Pavelka, Donna Kato, Louise Fischer-Cozzi, Tejae Floyde, Maria Belkomor, Larry Sanders, Christine Damm, Ellen
Prophater, Annie Pennington, Bettina Welker, Marcia Tzigelnik, Danielle Chandler, Doreen Kassel, Jan Montarsi; (spine)
Selena Anne Wells; (back cover, clockwise from top left) Genevieve Williamson, Katrin Neumaier, and Asvaneh Tajvidi

10 9 8 7 6 5 4 3 2 1

First Edition

Maggie Maggio, *Wrap Necklace*;
polymer; 120 x 2 inches (305 x
5cm). Photograph by Courtney
Frisse; modeled by Monica Maggio.
Inspiration for this series was drawn
from the neck rings worn by the
Ndebele women of South Africa.

Lynn Lunger, *Botanical Collection
Necklace*; polymer, ceramic wash-
ers, coconut shell, glass beads,
and sterling silver; 17 inches long
(43cm). Photograph by the artist.
The circular beads are based on
eucalyptus buds.

Genevieve Williamson, *Carved
Rings*; polymer; 1¼ inches (3cm).
Photograph by the artist. A solid
block of polymer with the center
removed makes for a seamless ring
and a smooth surface for carving.

Previous page: Juliya Lauhina,
Green and Blue Twisted Bangles;
polymer; 3 x 2 inches (7.5 x 5cm).
Photograph by the artist. This
young Russian artist sells her
wares at the Sunday market in
Moscow.

Acknowledgments

This is the awkward moment when I mumble my thank-yous, staring at the floor and swallowing hard. I am overwhelmed with gratitude.

Judy Belcher made book writing sound like the logical next step. She nipped at my heels, herding my doubts and keeping me on the path. My editor, Caitlin Harpin, and the staff at Random House assumed that I knew everything that was happening in the polymer world, and I strived to keep up with their expectations. I stood on the sidelines as Maggie Maggio and Lindly Haunani produced their wonderful book, *Polymer Clay Color Inspirations*. They told me that the process was like childbirth—a long gestation, the pain of delivery, and finally the joy of bringing an idea to life. Lindly told me when to push.

During the book's gestation friends and family listened patiently—at the Tuesday night ladies' Board of Directors meetings, at lunches with the McJam girls, during book club reviews, and at Saturday morning Breakfast Club confabs.

My daughter, Hillary, and I Skyped often and she gave honest feedback and gentle criticism. My son David and his wife, Tessa, continue to give me a glimpse into the world of fine art and academics. My sisters, Carol Lebeiko and Grace Christ, provided the therapy that only big sisters can supply. And I could always hear the voice of my late friend, Jan Crandell. I am glad that the early pieces of my polymer work that she loved to wear were returned to me after her death so that I could hide them.

I must acknowledge my good friends Skype, Photoshop, Dropbox, and Gmail. How did artists gather information before these tools became our pals?

My husband, Blair, gave me space and time and "you go, girl" enthusiasm. He has been my collaborator in art, life, and in this book.

My biggest thanks go to my generous readers. Thirteen of them were kind enough to tell their stories here and more than a hundred others offered their images. Thanks to all of you who follow along on PolymerClayDaily.com and join me in the pursuit of polymer art and inspiration.

Contents

Introduction

From the coasts of Canada to the mountains of Nepal, the artists in this book may be separated by geography and culture, yet they speak a common language through polymer. They represent a new generation of culturally diverse artists who are bringing enthusiasm and fresh perspective to the medium as they share their histories, values, and beliefs through their remarkable work. For them, polymer has been a way of changing a life, coping, coming out of a shell, speaking up, finding solace, and expressing their true selves. They have found friends across borders, a tribe of passionate enthusiasts, and a lifesaver in the opportunity to make and play with clay.

Melanie Muir, *Skye Line Necklace*; polymer; 24 inches (61cm). Photograph by Ewen Weatherspoon. This Scottish artist was inspired by the outline of the Cuillin Mountains on the Isle of Skye.

Introduced in the 1940s as a material for children, polymer clay continues to invite us to play. Indeed you will find that *play* is a theme throughout these artists' stories. But the current wave of polymer artists leapfrogs over the first generation's shy self-consciousness about using a medium that was originally intended as a toy for children. Unconcerned about polymer's history, they see it as portable, affordable, and endlessly adaptable—pure color that can be sculpted. Polymer can be a rock, a bead, a monster, a shrine, a bowl, a complex geometric pattern, and much more. Its chameleonlike properties allow an artist to express a unique vision. There's no other medium like it.

Even in the most remote areas, polymer artists are only a click away from each other. Since 2005, I have curated some of their most intriguing works on *Polymer Clay Daily*, a lifeline for anyone trying to stay in touch both with other artists and with the quick advancement of trends and techniques. Our community has flourished as the world becomes smaller, and the conversation on *Polymer Clay Daily* helps us keep our heads above the rising tide of information flooding in from a growing number of polymer-related sites.

This book gathers art from more than one hundred artists living and traveling all over the world, curated in thematic galleries that invite you to explore the world from your own polymer studio. Each of the thirteen artists featured in this book has an intriguing story, personal goals, and challenges to overcome. Some make art as their livelihood, some make for their own amusement or to help others, and others make in order to teach. In all cases, they wanted to share some of their signature techniques in project tutorials that transcend geographical and culture boundaries.

Because it is portable, polymer attracts artists whose lives require them to move frequently and who can't drag a studio full of equipment on their journeys. In this book, you'll read about ceramicists, glassblowers, and fiber artists

Wendy Moore, *Six Nepali Ladies*; polymer and glass beads;
3 inches tall (7.5cm). Photograph by the artist.

who have moved to polymer art because it travels well. With global markets and instant electronic access, today's artists can easily set up online galleries and reach a huge audience from anywhere.

While many of these artists share inspiring stories about their personal development from casual hobbyists to professional artists, this book isn't about how to get work into museums or how to succeed in business. It's about how to succeed with your art personally and measure success on your own terms. We have many amateur polymer artists, and that's a good thing. After all, the word *amateur* comes from the Latin word for "lover" and means creating for the sheer love of it. Exploration and personal growth are valid enough reasons to create.

As you peruse the galleries and read these artists' stories, listen to what they bring to their work, and observe how they tell their stories through the clay. You'll see how their art reflects, contradicts, or challenges their identities and cultures as they bring polymer to life. And more to the point, you'll learn how to pay attention to your own work, explore polymer clay techniques, and refine your vision to create work that stands out and articulates your unique perspective on the world. Look closely at what you make and you will learn about yourself. Your art is your signature.

A History of Polymer

EARLY BEGINNINGS

American artists had been dabbling with this German-made clay in new ways since the late 1980s, but Nan Roche gathered these major concepts and techniques into *The New Clay*, published in 1992. Notable polymer teachers, including Donna Kato and Maureen Carlson, began demonstrating easy and appealing clay projects on American television craft shows. Canadian artists soon took note and began to dabble in polymer as a serious medium, though it would take a few more years for the Canadian Polymer Clay Friends (or Clayamies) to form.

In the mid-1990s Donna Kato, working first for Polyform and later for Fimo, began traveling abroad at the request of clay distributors who were looking to sell more clay. Her demonstrations showed artists how to move beyond the small sculptures and miniatures that they were accustomed to. After several years of teaching the basic processes and designs, Donna began enlisting others to introduce color techniques and explore polymer more in-depth. Partially as a result of those demos, European enthusiasts began forming groups and guilds, and attending events in the United States. The guilds' collective resources also meant they could afford to invite more teachers overseas. Then these new groups began organizing their own events based on some of the American conferences: Clay Carnival in France, for example, was a spin-off of Donna's Clay Carnival in Las Vegas. American artists and teachers continued to have an influential presence abroad. Gwen Gibson and Louise Fischer Cozzi set up polymer workshops in their European residences. Helen Cox set up the first of many Polymer Carnivals that attracted participants from Spain and the Czech Republic. Polymer lends itself well to social gatherings, and interest grew as groups formed and guilds blossomed.

Donna Kato, *Pasha Ring*; polymer and gold leaf; 2 inches (5cm). Photograph by the artist.

Alice Stroppel and Meisha Barbee, *Collaborative Pendants*; polymer; 2 inches (5cm) and 3 inches (7.5cm). Photograph by Cynthia Tinapple. At a conference, Alice introduced her Stroppel cane; Meisha added dashes of color and texture.

RISE OF THE INTERNET

Online connections have been the heart of the polymer clay community for many years, ever since early sites such as Prodigy, AOL, and CompuServe first allowed artists' enthusiasm to transcend geographic boundaries. With the rise of the Internet and the subsequent growth of personal artists' blogs, the genie was out of the bottle! It's difficult in retrospect to track exactly how the trend spread, but having an online presence has been vital in helping many polymer artists find an audience as well as close polymer-artist friends.

I had been a member of the early online communities and editor for the National Polymer Clay Guild (later the International Polymer Clay Guild) in the 1990s. I wanted to ride the new wave of enthusiasm for the craft and began *Polymer Clay Daily* (*PCD*) as a blog in the fall of 2005. At first the majority of the traffic came from the United States and Canada, but soon nearly half of my readers came from 183 countries outside the United States. Since those early days, *PCD* has become a hub for artists to discover new techniques, share innovations, and develop a globalized style that defies conventional boundaries.

LIFE CYCLE OF A TECHNIQUE

Watching an idea migrate around the globe is one of the most fascinating features of blogging. I first knew that Alice Stroppel had a hot idea when I saw her at a conference gathering her scrap to make a usable cane by adding thin black layers. Artists are always looking for new ways to make good use of scrap! Alice released her tutorial online (and *PCD* linked to it), and within hours, experiments and variations began appearing on photo-hosting sites. Time zone by time zone, as readers woke to drink coffee and read the blog, they discovered photos of others' efforts. The variations continued more than a year later.

Bettina Welker, *Pixelated Retro Blend Bangle*; polymer; 3 x 4 inches (7.5 x10cm). Photograph by the artist.

Examples of this travel abound. Bettina Welker's extruded retro cane, Christine Dumond's hollow forms, Maggie Maggio's split rings, and Melanie West's big bio bangles all generated instant experimentation around the globe. For a technique to generate this kind of excitement requires three elements: It must be (1) a relatively simple process that (2) solves a problem and (3) offers possibility for morphing into a variation that an artist can call his or her own. Initially, artists simply duplicate the exercise and create many look-alikes. But they soon integrate the technique into their repertoire and give it their own flair.

INTERNATIONAL STYLE

Scanning hundreds of blogs each day, I often find that cultural and geographical lines are blurred. Polymer lends itself to a truly international style. A polymer article in Russian turns out to be written by an Israeli artist living in Brooklyn. While the acclaimed French teacher Cecelia Botton works in Hong Kong, the American artist Jon Anderson creates his sculptures in Bali. I can even tell when a particular teacher has been traveling just by tracking new art posted online that reflects their signature style.

Meanwhile, we have witnessed a global move away from obsessive consumerism toward more meaningful consumption as economies around the world have struggled. More than ever, people want to be engaged and inspired by what they buy. The international and technology-based movements celebrating crafts, do-it-yourself, and maker culture have promoted hands-on work. Buyers enjoy knowing that they've done their bit to help a craftsman and support a local economy. Even when they are buying online, polymer fans know that they're dealing with a human, not a machine.

Some of the most prominent communities and guilds now reflect this globalization. The National Polymer Clay Guild (NPCG), formed in 1989, attracted European artists to NPCG events, and it was clear that changing the name to include a wider audience would be necessary. In 2008 NPCG became the International Polymer Clay Association.

MUSEUM QUALITY

There was a time when museums shunned photography and when pottery was considered too utilitarian to have artistic value. The polymer community has recently challenged similar biases and overcome those obstacles.

In the last few years polymer has been accepted into major collections. Due to the diligence, vision, and persistence of Elise Winters and a crew of dedicated artists, several major museum shows have been mounted beginning in 2009 with the Fuller Craft Museum's *Sculpting Color* in Brockton, Massachusetts. In the fall of 2011 polymer shows opened concurrently in two museums: in Racine, Wisconsin, the Racine Art Museum collected works in *Terra Nova: Polymer Art at the Crossroads,* while an exhibit titled *New Jewelry in a New Medium* took place at the Mingei International Museum in San Diego, California. Through these efforts, polymer has shed its previous lowly status, and artists have come to expect that their work can be taken seriously in the art world.

The future for polymer art looks bright and global.

Cecelia Botton, *Orchids*; polymer; 16 inches (41cm). Photograph by the artist. Cecelia Botton is a French designer working in China.

Maggie Maggio, *Loosely Wound*; polymer. Photograph by Courtney Frisse; modeled by Monica Maggio.

Polymer Clay in a Nutshell

Before we begin our journey in polymer clay around the world, let's answer the most common questions about working in this medium, understanding the tools, working with the materials, and reviewing a few techniques that will be referred to later in the book. You can find more information about the suppliers of polymer clay and various tools in Resources (page 157). The polymer community generously shares information, so a simple Web search can provide answers to any questions not covered here.

POLYMER TOOLS
A WORD OF ADVICE

Refrain from purchasing too many supplies before you start. Your hands are the best tools, and shopping can overwhelm and divert you from the real fun of playing with clay. Most of the projects in this book call for just a few supplies, and you'll see that recommended brands of clay, tools, and other materials vary from artist to artist. You might even be surprised by what you can repurpose from your kitchen drawers, tool boxes, and sewing kits. When you want to delve more deeply into the polymer experience,

you can consider investing in a pasta machine, measuring tools, knives, carving and sculpting tools, shape cutters, drills, sandpapers, a clay extruder, and push molds.

There is plenty of time to invest in tools and advanced supplies and classes, so explore and experiment before you outfit your studio. Once you have an idea for the designs and techniques that express you best, you may find the perfect tools for your signature look in some unexpected sources, such as hardware stores, cake decorating suppliers, or even

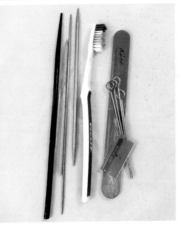

As I've explored polymer around the world, I've collected a variety of handmade tools invented by the artists who use them.

To work efficiently, Genevieve Williamson (page 75) begins by gathering the few tools she'll need for her design. A blade, work surface, and roller are key. Photograph by Genevieve Williamson.

fabric shops. I have collected tools from artists around the world, and I am delighted and surprised by the variety and creativity they employ in finding tools to cut, shape, and texture their clay.

TOOL KIT ESSENTIALS

As you begin to delve into the polymer experience, you'll need a few basic tools. While I encourage you to experiment to find what works best for you, these are the basic categories your tool kit will need to provide, with suggested examples for each.

Work surface: A smooth ceramic tile, piece of glass, or acrylic cutting board. Avoid working on wood, as polymer reacts with many types of wood finishes. Many people like to work on a glass, silicone, or ceramic surface that can be transferred directly into the oven. This minimizes disruption to the clay during the forming and firing process.

Roller: A rolling pin, dowel, brayer, acrylic rod, pasta machine, or straight-sided glass.

Cutter: A tissue blade, craft knife, or scalpel.

Sharp point: A needle tool or awl, large needle, wooden skewer, or toothpick to create the hole in beads and to

"scribe" designs, such as those etched into Rebecca Watkin's beads (page 137).

Shaper: A spoon or burnishing tool, bone folder, or clay-shaping tools. Your fingers will also work.

Texturizer: Rubber stamps, sandpaper, lace, or screws—anything that will make a mark is fair game. Wendy Moore uses a ceramic foot pumice to add texture to her beadwork (page 127).

Baking surface: Card stock, poster board, flame-retardant polyester quilt batting, or cornstarch (which creates a soft, matte surface for your work to rest on in the oven).

Storage: Plastic wrap, deli wrap or waxed paper, or plastic baggies. Some plastics, like CD jewel cases, will soak up the residual plasticizer and become softened by it. The plastic of sandwich bags seems to be inert. Not all plastic wrap is the same, so check your stored clay from time to time to see if it's reacting to its storage container.

Cleaning supplies: Isopropyl alcohol on a paper towel removes polymer residue from blades and other tools.

CLAY PROPERTIES AND TECHNIQUES

Polymer clay is an oven-baked modeling material composed of polymers, resins, coloring agents, and fillers. Unlike natural clay, it is made from a plastic, polyvinyl chloride (PVC) base. It has been used by both artists and hobbyists, from children to professional artists. Polymer clay can be used for jewelry, home decoration, scrapbooking, sculpture, miniatures, illustration, mosaics, baskets, dolls, and more. Polymer is a relatively new art medium, and part of its charm is that the frontiers are still being explored.

Polymer clay will not dry out, even when exposed to the air. It fuses into a hard, durable plastic when baked for approximately twenty minutes at a moderate temperature of 270° F (130° C). Polymer clay contains no water and is not mixable with water. It does not shrink perceptibly, and most colors remain true when baked. Available in many colors including metallic, glow-in-the-dark, and translucent varieties, with the right texturing tools and finishes polymer can simulate many materials, such as stone, porcelain, wood, textiles, glass, and more.

BRANDS TO LOOK FOR

Premo! Sculpey, Fimo, Kato Polyclay, Pardo, and Cernit are the most readily available brands of clay, but new companies and products are springing up as polymer grows in popularity around the world. Several manufacturers offer polymer clay in liquid form that can be used as an adhesive for polymer, or for layering and collaging effects. Each brand has slightly different properties with regard to elasticity, tensile strength, ranges of colors, and hardening temperatures. Kato Polyclay is regarded as the strongest clay; Premo and Fimosoft are the most elastic. Experiment with the clays available to you to determine the properties most important to your work, and choose accordingly.

Polymer clay brands are chemically similar and can be mixed together to customize color, reduce weight, or enhance stability. Keep in mind, however, that different brands cure at different temperatures, so it's best to limit yourself to one brand of clay if you want to eliminate concerns about temperature variations. If you mix two clays with different recommended temperatures, select the higher baking temperature to insure the integrity of the clay.

COLOR AND SPECIAL EFFECTS

Techniques for working with polymer have been borrowed from glassmaking, metalworking, ceramics, sculpture, and textiles. Clay can be used to cover frames, glass bases, pens, mirrors, metal forms and armatures—anything that will withstand the 270° F (130° C) firing temperature. Polymer can be used over baked forms made with Sculpey UltraLight clay to reduce the weight of a finished piece. For other complex shapes, some artists begin with two-part epoxy air-drying clay that they shape, dry, and cover with polymer before baking again.

Prepackaged colors can be combined to create custom colors by twisting and rolling the clays together until the colors have blended. To achieve special effects, the clay can be mixed before baking with powders, chalks, inks, glitters, embossing powders, powdered makeup, metal leaf, spices, and more.

After baking, polymer clay can be sanded, buffed, glazed, drilled, carved, drawn on, painted, and given a patina effect. Water-based acrylics or heat-set oil paints can be applied in several thin layers. Drawing with permanent pens, markers, and colored pencils will work, but these layers should be protected and preserved with a sealer such as PMY II.

Polymer can be modified, added to, and rebaked. For example, if you want to achieve a smooth, shiny finish, first bake the clay, let it cool, and then sand it with wet/dry sandpaper under running water. Buff the piece with a clean, soft cloth such as cotton or denim. Glazes, pastes, resins, or gloss paints may be applied after baking to enhance the shine. On more complex projects, it is not unusual to reheat the clay multiple times, baking after each step.

Sandra Trachsel, *Tumbling Blocks Bracelet*; polymer and glass beads; 6 x 2 inches (15 x 5cm). Sandra, who is from Germany, uses quilts as her reference for this cane.

Pasta Machine Settings

Throughout this book you'll see that playing cards are used to designate the recommended thickness of the clay in each step of every project. These notes indicate how many playing cards you would need to stack in order to achieve the desired thickness of clay.

This standard of measurement was invented when artists from all over the world responded to a Worldwide Pasta Machine Survey compiled in 2012 by Sage Bray, publisher of *The Polymer Arts* magazine, and Maggie Maggio. Readers in more than a dozen countries filled out the survey. The data showed that the consistency of polymer-sheet thickness produced from settings on different brands of pasta machines varied widely.

This method standardizes thickness settings whether you're rolling your clay by hand or with a pasta machine. Playing cards (which are universally the same thickness) can be inserted between the pasta machine's rollers. The results show what number of cards correlates with each setting on your particular brand of machine. I recommend writing these conversions on a chart (see below) and attaching it to your machine for each reference as you follow the projects.

As more teachers and publications begin to use this playing card guide to standardize thickness, students and readers will be able to produce more consistent results no matter what machine or roller they use anywhere in the world.

DESIGNATION	MILLIMETERS	# OF CARDS	PM SETTING
Extra Thick	3.0	9-10	#
Thick	2.5	7-8	#
Medium Thick	2.0	5-6	#
Medium	1.5	3-4	#
Medium Thin	1.0	1-2	#
Thin	.5	0-1	#
Extra Thin	< 0.5	0	#

SAFETY PRECAUTIONS

Casual clay hobbyists can safely bake the clay in their home ovens, taking care to properly ventilate. Artists who frequently bake generally use a toaster oven reserved for polymer firing only. Clay should not be used with anything that will subsequently touch food. Cookie sheets can be lined with foil, card stock, or index cards during baking. If you use kitchen items as clay tools, be sure that these do not return to food-preparation use. When working with clay, wash your hands frequently and especially before eating. Small children should be supervised when using this medium; while polymer clay is certified as nontoxic for ordinary use, it should not be ingested.

If you have concerns about the release of fumes during baking, you can bake clay in a sealed oven bag, or wash the inside of the oven with baking soda and water after baking your clay.

If your skin is sensitive, you may want to wear craft gloves to protect your hands. Gloves offer the added benefit of reducing fingerprints and enhancing smooth surfaces.

BEFORE YOU BEGIN

Storing Clay Raw polymer clay should be stored away from heat and sunlight. Do not leave the clay in your vehicle on a hot day or in direct sunlight. Once the packaging has been opened, it is best to wrap the clay in waxed paper or plastic wrap, and then store it in an airtight container. Do not store it in food storage containers that you plan to use for food in the future. Properly stored, the clay can remain usable for years.

Conditioning Conditioning is simply the process of warming and kneading the clay in preparation for use. All polymer clays must be conditioned prior to use to help realign the particles. Conditioning increases the clay's pliability as it is being sculpted and maximizes its tensile strength after baking. By kneading and stretching, the clays can be easily conditioned in a very short period of time.

If you are conditioning by hand, roll and twist the clay into a snake. Roll the snake out to twice its length and fold it in half and twist it into a ropelike shape. Keep rolling, twisting, and folding until the snake doesn't crack and resembles the consistency of pulled taffy.

Some of the stronger, stiffer clays can be conditioned with the help of a pasta machine. Cut the clay into thin chunks and feed them through the machine, rolling them into sheets. Fold and reinsert the creased edge back into the machine. Repeat until the clay becomes pliable and the edges are smooth, about twenty times. Small amounts of additional plasticizer, such as Mix Quick, diluent, or liquid clay, can be mixed with clay that has become too stiff. Many artists use a food processor dedicated to claywork to begin the mixing process. The machine blends and cuts the clay into a cottage cheese-like consistency. The friction of the food processor warms the clay and makes it easier to condition and roll out.

Conditioned clay should remain ready for immediate use for several weeks. It may need to be primed with a few twists of the snake or passes through the pasta machine before beginning your project.

Leaching If the clay is very soft and sticky, *leaching*, or removing, some of the plasticizer will make the clay stiffer and easier to manage. Roll out the clay and place it between sheets of plain white printing paper. Place a book or heavy weight on the top of the stack. In an hour or so you will find an oily residue on the paper, and your clay should be more pleasant to work with. Still too soft? Replace the paper with fresh sheets and stack the clay again. Repeat until the clay reaches the desired consistency.

BAKING CLAY

The clays vary in baking time, so always follow the instructions printed on the package of clay. Preheat your oven to the recommended temperature and bake the clay on card stock or a ceramic tile. I recommended using an oven thermometer to verify temperature, especially in small toaster ovens.

In some small electric ovens the top heating element comes on sporadically to regulate temperature. A layer of foil over the clay will prevent the hot element from scorching the clay.

After baking, allow clay to cool and fully cure before handling it.

SKINNER BLENDS

Skinner blending is a technique for combining polymer colors that you will see incorporated into many of the projects. Judith Skinner, a pioneering computer programmer, developed this method of blending flat triangles to produce gradations of color. Butting the two triangle shapes together, then rolling the piece through a pasta machine multiple times allows the colors to blend smoothly as the ratio of the two colors changes from left to right.

Skinner Blend in a Pasta Machine

1. For a basic blend, start with two thick (7-8 playing cards) squares of contrasting clay. Cut the squares into triangles and stack and join the triangles into two layers as shown. Smooth the center seam to join the clay so that the blend remains intact as you roll it through the machine.

2. Roll the sheet through the machine at the thick setting (7-8 playing cards).

3. Fold the sheet in half from bottom to top. Place the folded edge on the rollers and reroll. Remind yourself of the mantra, "More than one color must always touch the rollers" as you fold and blend. If you accidentally turn the sheet and

blend beginning with a solid-color edge, you'll end up with a nice, new solid color but no blend. You may want to move your thickness setting to medium thick (5-6 playing cards) to expedite the process.

4. Repeat this step until you achieve a blend as smooth as you desire. A smooth gradation requires at least thirty passes through the machine in my experience.

5. Once you're satisfied with the gradation, you may use the results in a variety of ways. If you want to make your gradation into a cane, give the clay a quarter turn so that it runs from dark to light. To do this, fold your clay into a strip. The white bar under my left hand in the photo is a magnetic "shark" from the Cutting Edge (Resources, page 157) that keeps my clay from spreading too wide. Roll the clay at a medium-thin setting (1-2 playing cards).

6. The resulting long strip of clay can be accordion-folded into a square cane or rolled into a round cane. The finished canes can be use in several projects. The round cane (left) may be used in Kim Korringa's Fairy Wing Earrings (page 149), while the square cane (right) can be used in Wendy Moore's Tibetan Tube Necklace (page 127).

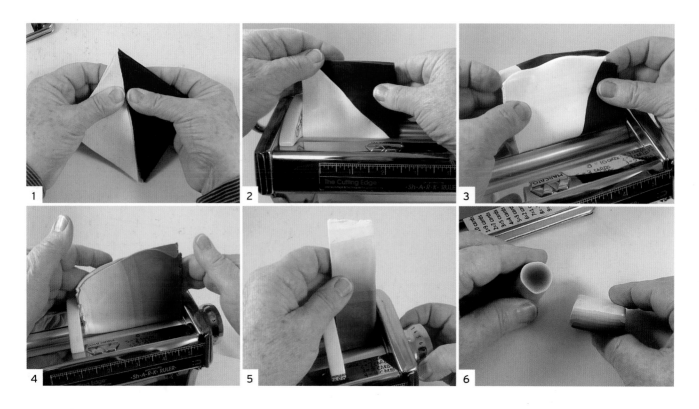

Manual Skinner Blend Making a Skinner blend by hand is part magic, part math. It may even give you more control over the outcome than a pasta machine allows. This method is especially good if you're dealing with a small amount of clay. Pasta machine versions can easily become misshapen and dog-eared, but your hands can stretch the clay into a more regular shape and make finer adjustments to the blend. What takes thirty to fifty passes through a pasta machine can be accomplished with far fewer by hand (five or six) rounds of twisting and rolling.

By folding or twisting two colors together in a consistent direction, the colors blend into each other. The concept was developed by Judith Skinner. The dimensions of the triangles will determine the ratio of the colors, while changing the geometry of the solid colors will produce varying gradations.

1. Start by conditioning and rolling out two thick (7-8 playing cards) 4-inch (10cm) squares of contrasting colors of clay. Cut both layers into triangles and reposition them into a stack. Pinch the center seams together. This helps keep the colors joined and aligned.

2. Roll the clay into a log.

3. Twist the log as if you were wringing out a wet towel. Roll and wring some more. After each wringing, the log will elongate. To keep the log from getting longer and thinner, push the ends toward the center. Maintain this fat cigar shape as you work.

4. Check your progress from time to time by flattening the log. Roll out the clay to see how the blend is beginning.

5. Reroll the clay into a log, making sure that you're keeping the same shape and twisting in the same direction. Repeatedly twist and roll into a cigar shape, checking your work by rolling it out from time to time.

6. When you flatten the clay, stretching it into a regular shape may help keep the blend under control. Five or six rounds of vigorous wringing and rolling will give you a very nice blend that's every bit as good as one made in a pasta machine.

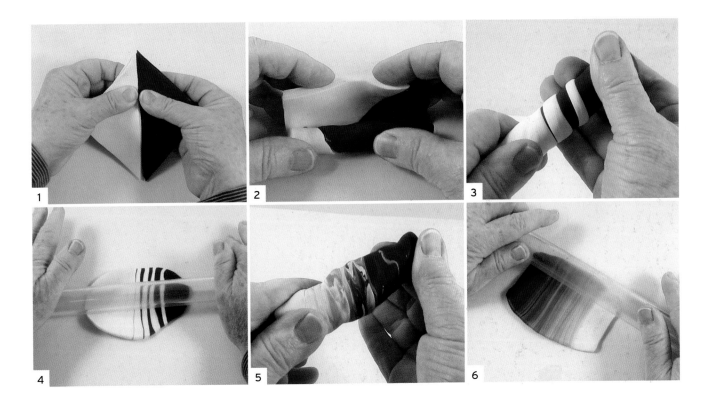

Assessing Your Work

A CHECKLIST FOR IMPACT

Every day as I research sites for my blog, *Polymer Clay Daily*, I flip through thousands of images in search of something that speaks to me, surprises me, or stops me in my tracks. As I'm automatically sifting and ordering, why do my eyes widen when I see a particular piece of art? Sometimes a compelling piece features only a rough-hewn approach or a simple technique. Other times, I may sense pain or joy or fear.

I don't have to understand what the artist intended in order to respond to it, but to help me make sense of my choices for *PCD*, I developed a checklist that you can also use to measure the effectiveness of your own work. There are four ingredients to my method. I have found that a successful piece must contain some combination of each of the four ingredients, even if it registers low in three parts and flies off the chart in the fourth. Keep in mind, a successful piece is never simply the result of following a formula; as in any recipe, it's the special blending of ingredients that adds the flavor.

THE INGREDIENTS

Energy When polymer shows an artist's playful energy, viewers take notice. Again and again, artists have told me that when they are stuck, play is the way out. We are lucky to be working with a material that has been considered a child's toy because our approach can naturally be more playful than what other, more serious mediums require.

How much energy or passion do you bring to your work? Are you allowing yourself to play when you create?

Mood We may react to humor, joy, sadness, anger, fear, or uncertainty in a piece. If the artist felt angst in making a bead, more often than not a viewer can sense it. On the flip side, a vibrant pendant might bring a smile to his or her face.

Is your piece dark, bright, colorful, happy? What spirit have you baked into your clay? Can you describe the mood you were in while creating the piece?

Esterke Raz, *Time Flies*; polymer and clock mechanism; 9 x 9 inches (23 x 23cm). Photograph by the artist. The colors, patterns, and slightly off-kilter angles give this wall clock by an Israeli artist a boisterous energy.

Sarah Wilbanks, *Midnight Grackle*; sterling silver, polymer, and image transfers; 2 x 3 inches (5 x 7.5cm). Photograph by the artist. Seattle-based artist Sarah's fine silver work, along with her use of ephemera and image transfers, creates a mysterious mood.

Ponsawan Silapiruti sometimes teases the viewer. When a friend joked that watermelon rinds were pretty enough to wear, Ponsawan made her a polymer version as part of her 2010 "Ring a Day" project. Photograph by the artist.

Canadian Joan Tayler sculpts each species' markings and shapes into the polymer and includes a descriptive list with each strand of birds. Influenced by her years living in Japan, Joan's work reminds the viewer to look closely at the beauty of nature. Photograph by Cynthia Tinapple.

Skill Evidence of technical skill will make a piece stand out immediately. We shake our heads in amazement when a piece is skillfully rendered. But there is a trade-off between perfection and expression, and sometimes fine pieces emerge when artists stop focusing on technique in order to pursue something deeper.

Did you finish your piece to a level that satisfies you? How important was technical prowess to the intent of this piece?

Innovation Copying masters' works is an old and honored tradition in art, and most people find their own voice only after they have tried sounding like a lot of others. But a piece that gives a new solution to a long-standing problem or new life to an old technique captures our attention. As you'll see, the Internet has become a playground for innovation, where a new technique quickly morphs as it is picked up around the globe.

How can you mix old ways with the new? Are you creating art that only you could create?

HOW DID THINGS GO WRONG?

Sometimes things can go wrong when one of the ingredients is missing. Lots of technical skill but no innovation falls flat. Lots of attitude but no energy won't be very satisfying. Instead of simply repeating yesterday's design, try exploring the questions in the checklist.

If you look at the works of artists you admire, you'll see that over the years the threads of their stories gain the strength of continuity. Their aesthetic becomes more clearly understood when the works eventually form a group. Keep working, and keep making art even when things go wrong. When things are good, make art. When things get bad, make art.

OTHER INFLUENCES

In addition to energy, mood, skill, and innovation, other layers of influences may loom large as artists pick up the clay. Geographical, political, and cultural factors, as well as age, income, and health, bring their own biases to bear. While I'll often get the particulars wrong (especially when it comes to the age or health of the artist), I'm rarely off the mark about the message or story that the artist wanted to tell through the work. I'm moved when readers make a special plea for their work because they come from a country that's undergoing upheaval. "Please don't think badly of me," they will beg. "My country is a mess." I'm also surprised when a new design that I imagined coming from a thirtysomething comes instead from a sixtysomething. There's nothing more fun for me than to fall in love with a piece, develop a story about its maker in my head, and then hear the actual story.

CATEGORIES OF MOTIVATION

I've talked with many artists who quote their Myers-Briggs test scores to explain their methods. For them, it's reassuring to see how their work is related to their broader perspective on life. As I started to explore the general personalities and motivations of the polymer artists I had encountered, I discovered five distinct categories to explain what inspired these artists.

Not everyone fell neatly into one category, but after talking with most of the artists in this book, I came away with the general sense that "she's a problem solver" or "he's a communicator." The words they used and the way they talked about their approach to work provided big clues about what pulled them into their studios. Understanding your own personality and motivations can help you understand what aspects of making bring you the most joy. Consider what motivates you to create. Think about how your personality and goals may be reflected in polymer.

THE PROBLEM SOLVERS

Problem solvers are driven by the need to bring order, find answers, and control outcomes. These are often the people who have come to art through the sciences and bring a structured, logical approach to their craft as well. "At what point do colors get muddy? Why does the clay crack?" they ask themselves as a starting point. For example, color expert Maggie Maggio (who is both a problem solver and an experimenter) pursues new solutions to exploit the plastic properties of polymer clay rather than trying to imitate other media. Other problem-solving artists are solving their own personal dilemmas. They may make art to stretch a creative muscle, to lose weight, or to stay busy during stressful times.

THE EXPERIMENTERS

Experimenters can't resist asking, "What if?" The grass is always greener in the next project. While they resemble problem solvers, experimenters' methods may be much less exact and much more carefree. They simply delight in seeing what is over the next horizon. Often these folks grew up in families where art was the focus, and as a result they are less constrained in their thinking. Take Pier Voulkos as an example of an experimenter. Both her parents were artists, and her father was the famous ceramicist Peter Voulkos. Pier was a pioneer in using polymer as an art material because her curiosity continually led her to question what was possible with the material.

Maggie Maggio, *Split Ring Necklace*; polymer; 24 inches (61cm). Photograph by Courtney Frisse; modeled by Monica Maggio. Maggie wants to exploit the properties of polymer instead of imitating other media. Her split rings illustrate polymer's flexibility and strength.

Pier Voulkos, *Potato Chip Bead Neckpiece*; polymer; 30 inches (76.2cm). Photograph by Cynthia Tinapple. An early experimenter, Pier explored chatoyant patterning on flat, ⅛-inch thick (3mm) beads that are built over slender precured tubes.

Dr. Ron Lehocky's 20,000 polymer heart pins have raised more than $200,000 for the Kid's Center in Kentucky. His work connects him with the community and gives him a format to explore. He's a socializer and a disciplinarian.

THE NATURALS

Artists who "flow," or operate from a stream of consciousness, mystify us. We envy their unedited and seemingly unfettered march to the studio. There's something that they must express, and no critic, no standard procedure, no rules will stop them from saying what they need to say. They do not analyze while they work, and the intensity and meaning of the finished work often surprise them. Art is the way they work out emotional issues. For them, art is a true voice and not one they can necessarily control. It is, however, a powerful approach, and we see that power in the earthy, personal works of polymer artist Leslie Blackford.

Most naturals grew up surrounded by art as a valuable and integral part of life, so they are less likely to question motives or edit expressive impulses.

THE DISCIPLINARIANS

Disciplinarians create boundaries, tasks, and lists to provide measures of comfort as they come to their work. That is not to say that their work isn't loose and inspired. Rather, they need a structure in which they can operate freely. They enjoy giving themselves permission, and they take pleasure in seeing the checkmarks on their lists. Dayle Doroshow, for example, will tell herself she must make five examples of each new idea in order to motivate her to follow through on a spark of inspiration.

THE SOCIALIZERS

Socializers make connections through their art, and they work in order to share. There's nothing better than an exhibit or a conference or a swap to get their creative juices flowing. Art is their ticket to a party, and when they're stuck, they turn to their sister and brother artists for help. They feel most motivated when they are collaborating with others, organizing events, and sharing their progress.

Socializers often see their work more as one piece of a bigger movement or conversation. Judy Belcher fits this bill, and she explores the power of collaboration in her book *Polymer Clay Master Class.*

After she saw a performance of *The Lion King*, Leslie Blackford began quickly sculpting the characters that filled her head. As a natural, she rarely preplans a piece, allowing her fingers to do the talking.

Judy Belcher's *IPCA Earrings* are a polymer version of the International Polymer Clay Association's logo. Traveling, teaching, and organizing motivate her work.

CHAPTER 1

Fashion Forward

Polymer easily lends itself to creating adornments, whether for yourself or for your home. Artists who draw from their personal stories, combined with their technical expertise, are creating some of the most vibrant, stylish pieces in this medium. "Fashion forward" means more than just the latest trend or current popular taste. The melding of the artist's philosophy, personality, and cultural perspective allows true style to blossom. Eva Haskova's work embodies a young Czech vibe that she thought was missing from jewelry available in the stores. Meanwhile, Fabiola Pérez Ajates creates jewelry and home decor with idiosyncratic methods that she developed on her own as she struggled to connect with the world around her. Polymer fans enjoy knowing the artists and welcome their personal connections to these stories.

Opposite, clockwise from top left:

Betsy Baker, *Dot Duo Pendants*; polymer, sterling silver, and image transfers; 1¾ inches (4cm). Photograph by the artist. Polka dots are always a fashion favorite. These pendants open up to reveal grids of sterling silver bubbles on red and green backgrounds.

Claire Wallis, *Bright Stripe Bangle*; polymer; 6 x 1 inches (15 x 2.5cm). Photograph by the artist. These bangles from the United Kingdom wobble for an interesting design, which the artist freely shares on-line. The purple form is baked, then the inside striped-and-pink layers are added, shaped, and baked again. Color-blocking trends and timeless black-and-white accents inspired her.

Angela Garrod, *Secesson Necklace*; polymer with gold mica and silver findings. Photograph by the artist. A member of the London Polymer Clay Group, this British artist creates tidy Bauhaus-like designs on hollow lentil beads for a very modern appeal.

Iris Mishly, *Skyscraper Bracelet*; polymer clay and metallic powders; 2 inches (5cm). Photograph by the artist. The long, narrow beads have a metallic sheen that reminded this Israeli artist of the New York skyline. Iris bakes the base shape and adds color later with liquid clay and powders.

Jennifer Parrish, *Gothic Fleur de Lis Crown*; polymer, agate stones, and freshwater stones; 6 inch diameter by 2 inches (5cm). Photograph by artist. Jennifer's polymer relics have appeared in many television, theater, and movie productions, including *Harry Potter and the Order of the Phoenix*. She also designs historic pieces for museum exhibitions as well as a line of handcrafted jewelry.

Loretta Lam, *Raspberries in May Necklace*; polymer, 18 inches (45.5cm). Photograph by the artist. Loretta is influenced by the natural forms found in her home in upstate New York to create oversized, yet featherweight, fashion jewelry.

Oksana Volkova, *Fashion Bangles*; polymer; 6 x 3 inches (15 x 7.5cm) each. Photograph by the artist. Oksana photographed her big polymer bangles and other beads on this Russian model in 2010. She has a flair for bold, outrageous fashions and colors. Polymer is well suited for her aesthetic and mixes well with contemporary knitted and felted accessories.

Céline Bateau-Kessler, *Mosaic Earrings*; polymer and crystals; 1 inch diameter (2.5cm). Photograph by the artist. Céline often bases her polymer palette on the latest French fashions. Slices of small canes are arranged into a pattern and fuse into one flat bead when baked, while crystals form the center of these dangling flowers.

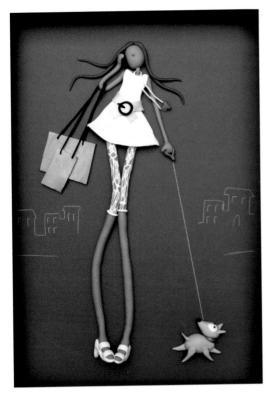

Françoise Guitton, *Romane*; polymer; 12 x 16 inches (30.5 x 41cm). Photograph by the artist. Graphic artist Françoise's polymer illustrations of fashion plates, such as this French shopper with her little dog, are each framed in a shadow box. Romane's elongated legs in lacy tights and flying hair add to her chic appeal.

Marina Lombardi, *Italian Beauty Necklace*; polymer, beads, glass, crystals, and wire; 24 inches (61cm). Photograph by the artist. The focal cabochon shows the face of a Botticelli maiden, framed by poppies and leaves in polymer with seed beads and red crystals on twisted wire. The colors, which echo those of the Italian flag, are a tribute to Marina's country.

Silvia Ortiz de la Torre, *Stomas Necklace*; polymer; 30 inches (76.2cm). Photograph by the artist. Riotous colors take a fashion leap in this design, based on techniques developed by fellow Spanish artist Natalia García de Leániz.

"I was searching for
something that would
take my heart." —EVA HASKOVA

Eva Haskova

The Eastern Bloc ▸ Prague. Czech Republic

It's difficult for Westerners to appreciate how much political changes in the Czech Republic have shifted attitudes about art and self-expression. Artists in the Eastern Bloc have become less influenced by the cultural imperatives of the communist state thanks to open borders, rising consumerism, and the free market of postcommunist Europe. As a young artist in this environment, Eva Haskova attended polymer events in neighboring countries, which exposed her to new possibilities.

Eva describes her past artistic pursuits—before polymer— as too flat, too virtual, or too complex. "I had tried lots of different disciplines. I studied graphic design and art therapy. I considered fashion design, stage design, and even conceptual art," she says. She grew up in a small arts-friendly family with a mother who teaches art, English, and Czech, and a father and younger brother who are both photographers. She knew that she was also destined to do something creative, but she wasn't hooked by anything she had tried. "I was searching, or waiting for something that would take my heart."

Polymer, which she discovered in 2007, offered that path. A year later, Eva went to the first Euro Clay Carnival in the United Kingdom, organized by Helen Cox. Meeting other polymer artists had a powerful effect on her. Before the carnival, the idea of making a living at clay had never occurred to her, but after the conference she could think of nothing else. "Art never leaves my mind," she admits. "I started buying clay to make myself jewelry that I could wear because I couldn't find what I liked in the shops."

She loves the freedom to express herself that polymer offers. "The longer I sit in my studio, the better the ideas that come to me. I don't plan, I play. In polymer clay I have found a connection between my favorite bits from other disciplines: playing with color, which never matched what was in my head when I was painting; sculpting, which too often forced me to make compromises; and graphic design, whose simple forms and clarity appealed to me, but was too virtual. I missed touching the art with my bare hands."

Even though there is a renewed interest in crafts, Eva contends that Czechs aren't used to paying money for hand-made items, which is why she needs to combine teaching and writing with jewelry sales to make a living. Eva teaches eight to ten classes a month in a shared arts facility and contributes articles to their magazine. Most of her students are older women who couldn't buy goods under communism and were forced to make everything by hand, including clothes, furniture, and even machinery. "They were used to creating and making things by hand, but now it's not so necessary, and they can turn those skills into artistic disciplines. They welcome the chance to work with their hands again, and polymer is very easy for them," she explains.

Eva's style is highly personal. Her preferred color palette draws from traditional Czech colors but with a modern edge that's all her own. Although she has a strong online presence, Eva professes an aversion to computers. She doesn't spend time looking at others' work online because she fears that that would affect her design sense. She prefers to travel to other polymer events around Europe whenever she can.

Opposite, clockwise from top left:

Eva in her Prague studio.

This polymer bangle and neckpiece update traditional Czech designs.

Eva combines dimensional elements and built-in bezels with her hollow pendant designs.

Alternating black-and-white cane patterns mingle on this bangle and beads.

Her mix of polymer patterns resonate with contemporary Czech culture.

Project:
Colorful Rays Spiral Pendant By Eva Haskova

Small slivers of Skinner blends are rearranged into glowing rays radiating out from a center spiral. By alternating the blends and using color strategically, Eva's design draws the eye in, compelling you to make sense of the shifting patterns. Because the domed shape is filled with air, the pendant is lighter than you would expect, and Eva's rich color palette reflects the influence of her heritage.

TOOLS AND MATERIALS

polymer clay (Fimo Classic) in translucent white, black, champagne, metallic gold, dark green, and bordeaux, plus scrap clay

pasta machine

silver foil leaf (or any other metal)

dry, clean brush for smoothing the foil

alcohol inks (red, orange, or green are the best for this project)

cotton swabs for dabbing inks

tissue blade

acrylic block or small, flat tile

glass or tile work surface

acrylic roller

fine- or medium-grained sponge for texturing

round cutter, the size of the finished pendant (sample is 2¾ inches [7cm])

100-grit sandpaper

U.S. size 8 (5mm) metal knitting needle

permanent pen or marker

craft knife

liquid polymer clay

small brush for applying liquid polymer

cord for hanging the pendant

INSTRUCTIONS

1 First make the small center spiral of the pendant. It's easiest to shape the spiral from a small stack of clay. Make the small stack by rolling out the translucent clay in the pasta machine at the thin setting (1 playing card). Stretch the clay thinner with your hands and set it aside. Condition the black clay. Prepare 2 layers of black clay rolled on the thick setting (7-8 playing cards) on a pasta machine. Cut out two rectangular strips about 1½ x 2 inches (3.8 × 5cm). Stack the 2 layers and lay the silver foil leaf on top. Smooth the surface of the metal leaf onto the clay with a clean dry brush, making sure that the foil has stuck.

2 Apply a few drops of several different colors of inks onto the top of the metal foil stack and smear the inks with a cotton swab so that any drops and puddles of ink are dispersed. Let the inks dry. (You can use any color of metal foil, add more inks, or omit them completely.)

3 Cover the metal foil and ink surface with the thin sheet of prepared translucent clay and smooth with your fingers to release any trapped air. Send the stack through the thick setting (7-8 playing cards) on your pasta machine.

4 Roll out another layer of black on the thick setting (7-8 playing cards) on the pasta machine and add this layer to the bottom of the stack. Bend the tissue blade slightly to cut the stack of clay and foil into long tear-drop shapes, approximately 2 inches (5cm) long and ¼ inch (6mm) wide. You can experiment with several sizes and later decide which one best suits the center of your pendant. Shape these narrow cutouts into spirals, and bake for 15 minutes at the manufacturer's recommended temperature.

1

2

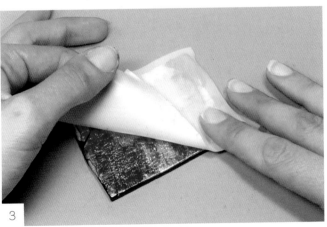

4

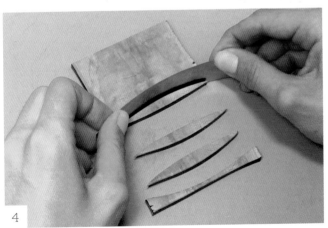

3

5 Separately condition the entire amount of champagne, gold, and green, and half of the bordeaux at the thickest setting on the pasta machine and arrange the clay as shown. Roll the sheet at the thick setting (7–8 playing cards) on the pasta machine until the colors are blended. Cut the prepared Skinner-blended sheet in half. Roll one half through the pasta machine at the medium-thick setting (5–6 playing cards), rotating the clay 90 degrees from its original direction.

6 Cut the Skinner-blended sheet as shown. Trim the edges, and then cut the piece into equal 4 parts. Cut these 4 parts cut into strips approximately ¼ to ½ inch (6 to 13mm) wide. It is good to have a variety of thick and thin strips. Then cut all the strips diagonally to create triangles. I used 23 triangles for the sample pendant.

7 Prepare a thin sheet of scrap clay at a medium setting (3–4 playing cards) on the pasta machine. Arrange the blended triangles into a circle, as shown in the photo. Maintain the straight edges of the triangles, pushing a stiff blade against their sides to keep them straight. After assembling the complete pattern, smooth the surface by rolling it with an acrylic roller in different directions, and then texturize the entire surface with a sponge.

8 Prepare a sheet of scrap clay at a medium-thick setting (5–6 playing cards) on the pasta machine. Line up the round cutter with the middle of the pattern. Being

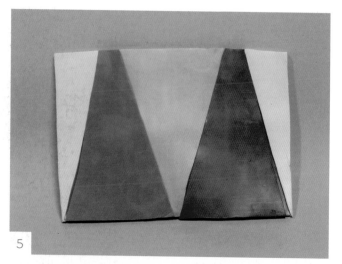

5

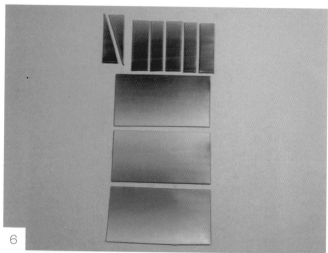

6

7

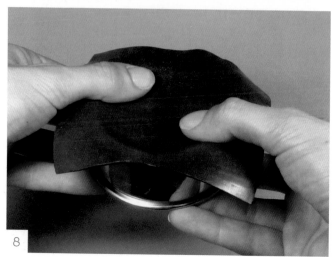

8

careful not to cut the clay completely yet, gently press the cutter against the surface of the pattern. Flip the clay and cutter upside down. The back of the patterned sheet is now facing up. Sculpt it gently with your fingers to create a convex shape.

Flip the cutter and clay over again onto a sheet of scrap clay. Press the cutter through both the patterned sheet and scrap clay sheet. This traps a pocket of air and forms the nice convex shape of the pendant.

9 Choose one of the conditioned solid colors to create an accent for the middle of your pendant. In the sample, I mixed green and gold for the accent. Flatten a small ball of this color into a disk. Texturize the accent disk with a sponge or sandpaper. The spiral you made in step 4 will be placed on top of this solid-colored disk.

Join the spiral and the accent disk together with liquid polymer, adjusting the edges of the disk so that the color shows around the spiral.

10 Gently press the spiral and accent into the middle of the pendant to adhere it. Bake for 20 minutes at the manufacturer's recommended temperature.

11 To create the hanger, prepare a sheet of scrap clay at the thick setting (7–8 playing cards) and as wide as the pendant. Wrap one layer around a knitting needle to form a tube.

12 With a permanent pen or marker, draw 2 lines the same width as the tube on the back of the baked pendant to show where the hanger should be placed.

9

10

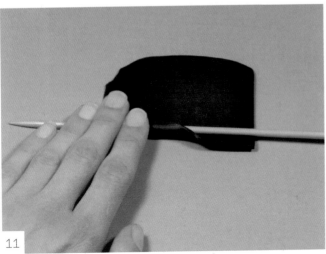

11

12

13 With a craft knife, carefully cut the baked clay along the drawn lines. Carve this section out, being careful not to cut too deeply or disturb the front of the pendant.

14 Coat this cutout area with liquid polymer and gently press the tube created in step 11 into the gap. Be careful not to distort the tube, which should extend ½ inch (13mm) beyond the pendant on each side. Bake for 20 minutes.

15 After baking, cut off the overhanging sections of the tube with a craft knife so that the ends are even with the pendant. Sand the tube ends to make them as flush as possible.

16 Prepare a thick sheet of scrap clay and cut it to the pendant size with the same round cutter. Using a tissue blade, eliminate the strip where the tube was inserted. Cut another layer of scrap clay in 2 pieces to fit on each side of the tube.

Coat the back of the pendant with a thin layer of liquid polymer. Place the pieces of prepared scrap so they line up and smooth them into place. Trim the edges of the unbaked clay with your craft knife.

Bake for 15 minutes.

13

14

15

16

17 Sand the back and sides of the baked pendant a bit if necessary.

Mix the remaining bordeaux clay with the scraps of black clay left over in step 1. Roll this darker bordeaux shade through the medium setting (3-4 playing cards). Texture the sheet with the sponge and cut a circle with a cookie cutter about ¼ inch (6mm) larger than the pendant.

Cover the back of the pendant with liquid polymer and press the textured bordeaux circle onto the back with the textured side facing outward. Smooth from the middle to the edges, squeezing out any air bubbles.

Curve the edges around the sides of the pendant. Touch up the texture with the sponge or sandpaper.

18 Trim any overhanging clay with a craft knife. Repeat this pressing, cutting, and texturing until the back and edges look finished.

19 Reopen the holes where the pendant will hang by gently inserting the knitting needle into the tube. Bake for 30 minutes.

17

18

19

"What I feel is transferred to the clay through my hands." —FABIOLA PÉREZ AJATES

Fabiola Pérez Ajates
Speaking Without Words ➤ Madrid, Spain

From the confines of my quiet world I have struggled to remain open and to integrate myself into society," says Fabiola Pérez Ajates. "Though I've been totally deaf since birth, that has not kept me from living a fulfilling life, and I have a rich imagination." The shapes that Fabi creates in clay have an endearing looseness and playful attitude. To these shapes she applies color in unexpected ways. The pieces almost dance with abandon, colorful dishes stacked so that one's edges curl up over the next.

Fabi grew up making art and all her own jewelry, and she especially enjoyed creating items to decorate and be useful at home. Later, when she was plagued by strong migraines, art helped calm and relax her. "I grew up in a small Spanish village and remember feeling happiest surrounded by animals—cats, dogs, rabbits, donkeys," she recalls. "I went to school later than the other children, and I was often alone. The animals understood me better than the people who saw me only as mute and deaf. I still feel a deep love for animals." While Fabi works with all kinds of materials and techniques, polymer allows her to give shape to her inner world in bold colors. "What I feel is transferred to the clay through my hands. This is my voice, not heard but seen. I've always collected boxes, which I fill with my collections of small photos, fossils, and jewelry. Even though I may not remember exactly why I collected them, I am happiest surrounded by these small treasures."

Discovering polymer in a local craft store in 2009, she immediately signed up for lessons. Fabi quickly learned the basics and wanted more, so she scoured the Internet for information and found inspiration in the works of favorite artists like Kathleen Dustin, Lindly Haunani, and Sarah Shriver. "Artists' websites provided a visual encyclopedia of techniques and ideas," she says. "The Web opened a window on the world for me." Online exploration was less stressful for her than attending overstimulating polymer events and gatherings in Spain.

Her friends joined her for informal classes, and as word spread, more people were interested. "Initially I had difficulty communicating with students, but I am very stubborn and I wouldn't give up. When I see my students' wonderful works I feel a great satisfaction knowing that I am understood and appreciated. My students are thrilled with the beautiful pieces they've made." Her students' work is impressive, a testament to Fabi's teaching skills.

She set up her own classroom workshop, created an online gallery for her art and tutorials, and began working with a craft store in Malaga. She also began taking commissions. Her polymer mosaic portrait of her son was quickly spotted by other artists on the Web. She expanded her portraiture and is working on developing new techniques and taking commissions.

Fabi adds, "Teaching has allowed me to share what I know with other people and to see the world through someone else's eyes."

Opposite, clockwise from top left:

Fabi works and teaches workshops in her home studio in Madrid.

Her decorative plates are embellished with unusual stamps and patterns, which are accented by washes of color.

By rolling scrap colors into thin sheets and saving them, Fabi accumulated the pieces she needed for this polymer mosaic of her son. Only the white shirt pieces were from fresh clay.

Fabi continually experiments with the shape and the legs of her plates. The textures beg to be touched.

Floral Pendant By Fabiola Pérez Ajates

It's surprisingly easy to learn the carving methods that created the simple, graphic shapes in this pendant. You may be equally surprised to see that the ombré rainbow palette actually begins with a bright wasabi-colored base of Premo. Fabiola has devised a method for hanging her pendants that assures a perfect fit with no drilling required.

TOOLS AND MATERIALS

Premo! Sculpey polymer clay in ecru, white, green wasabi, and gold
paper and pencil for sketching
scissors
pasta machine
tile
craft knife
pen
gouge with several tips
talcum powder
wooden skewer
small flood light bulb
blade
scalpel
paintbrushes
acrylic paint in violet and green
several soft cotton cloths
Translucent Liquid Sculpey
cord for hanging the pendant
leather twine or string
sandpaper or texture template
Renaissance Micro-Crystalline Wax Polish or Armor All
brushes for applying wax
piece of denim for polishing

INSTRUCTIONS

1 On paper, sketch the outline of the desired pendant shape and cut out the pattern. To create the mold for your raised design, condition a piece of neutral-colored clay (in the sample I've mixed ecru with a little white) through the pasta machine at the thick setting (8 playing cards). Place the clay on a tile with the paper pattern on top. Cut the clay in a rectangular shape at least as large as your pattern. Bake this rectangle of clay on the tile for 25 minutes at the manufacturer's recommended temperature.

2 With the pen, draw your design on the rectangle of baked Premo. Then use the triangular gouge tip to carve furrows along the lines you've drawn.

3 This rectangular piece with the carved design will be used as a mold.

4 Brush the baked mold with a bit of talcum powder. Run the wasabi clay through the pasta machine on the thick setting (8 playing cards). Press the clay onto the carved mold with your fingers. To make the pendant sturdier, add another layer of wasabi, conditioned so that it is slightly thinner than the first layer (6 playing cards). Press the thinner sheet onto the pendant base.

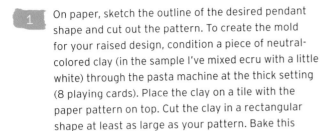

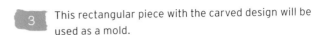

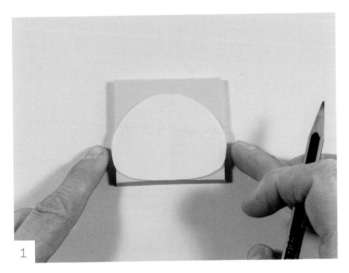

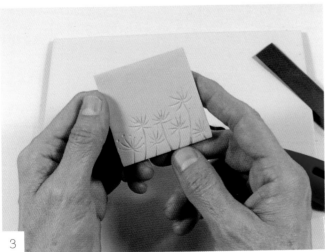

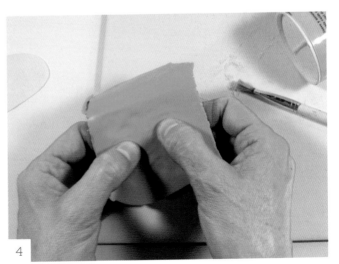

5 Carefully separate the carved mold from the wasabi Premo, making sure the image is crisp and clear.

6 Determine which area of the image works best for your pendant. Using the paper pattern as a guide and a craft knife, cut your stamped clay into the pendant shape.

7 Transfer the stamped clay to a light bulb, which will support the piece and give the pendant a gentle convex shape while tolerating the heat of the oven. Make several tiny balls of the same color clay and position the balls at the end of the lines using a skewer. Gently push down on the balls to make them adhere. Trim any rough edges on the basic shape. Bake in the oven for 15 minutes. Remove it and wait for it to cool. Using the scalpel to pry an edge, remove the piece from the light bulb.

8 Wet the tip of the brush with water and quickly paint the top portion of the surface with violet acrylic paint. Dab it with the cloth to reveal a bit of the clay color.

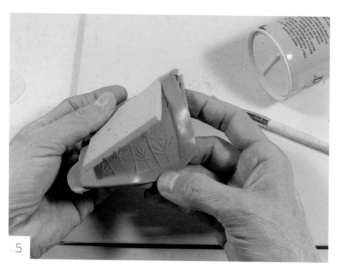

5

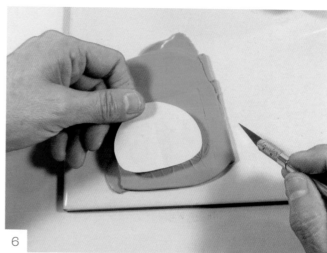

6

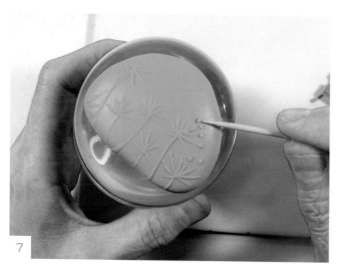

7

8

9 Do the same at the bottom of the piece with the green acrylic paint. Wet the tip of the brush with a little water and then paint on the green. Quickly dab the paint with the cloth.

10 Gently mix the area where the two colors meet with a cloth until it looks good to you. Repeat as you like to darken the colors and achieve a nice gradient. Once you're satisfied, let the piece air dry for 1-2 hours.

11 Moisten the cotton cloth and gently rub the raised pattern to remove enough paint to reveal the original wasabi color on the raised areas. If the paint sticks too much, use a cutter or knife to scrape off some of the paint.

12 Cover the back of the piece with liquid clay and another layer of contrasting clay, trimming the edges with a blade to make a smooth surface. Using the cord on which you intend hang the pendant, choose the best placement for the cord. When you've chosen how the pendant will be aligned on the cord, press the cord into the clay to make an indentation.

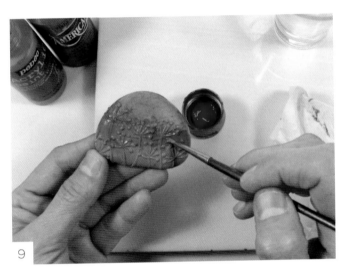

9

10

11

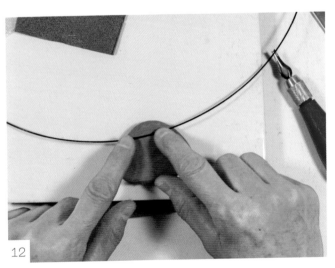

12

13 The cord will leave a curved shape, but we are only interested in the points where the cord enters and exits the pendant. With a cutting blade, mark a straight line connecting the entrance and exit points. With a semicircular gouge cut the straight line in the unbaked clay on the back of the pendant.

14 Insert a short length of leather twine or string in the line you've just carved to keep the hole open while you add the back. Roll the gold clay through the pasta machine on the medium-thick setting (5 playing cards) and add texture to this layer with sandpaper or the tool of your choice. Place the gold clay on the back of the pendant and trim around the edges with a blade. Touch up the texture as needed and make sure that the twine moves freely in the hole. Bake the entire piece (with the twine in place) in the oven for 15 minutes. When it has cooled, remove the twine, add Renaissance wax or Armor All over the entire piece with a brush or by hand. Let the wax dry a bit. Gently buff the surface with a cotton cloth and then with a piece of denim for a glossy finish.

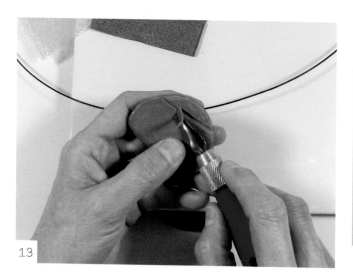

13

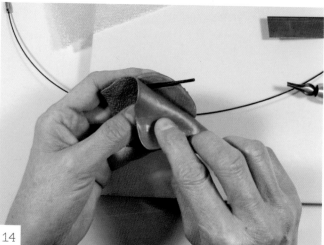

14

Vive la Différence

American teachers abroad report surprisingly few translation difficulties. If students can see the teacher's hands, they can understand. American teachers are sometimes startled by the enthusiasm of a younger, thinner, and very technically competent audience.

Says one seasoned American traveling instructor, "The opportunity for using the workshop as a therapeutic session, a cathartic event, or a time for introspection hasn't occurred to Europeans. There is a willingness to evolve and a desire to bring their own design-related decisions to the project that is being demonstrated. There's less of an attempt to try to please the instructor and more of an 'I can do it' attitude. In forums such as Voila's online class, How to Become a Better Artist, members are much more willing to accept criticism with a kind of vulnerability, sensibility, and candor rare in the United States. On the other hand, what we in the United States would consider blatant copyright and intellectual property trespasses are easily tolerated in some parts of the world."

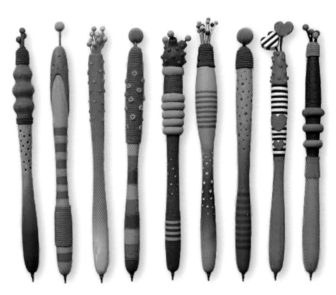

Jana Lehmann, *Skinner Blend Pens*; polymer; 7 inches (18cm). Photograph by the artist. German artist Jana Lehmann has a distinctive graphic style that works particularly well on pens. She covers the wooden forms with Skinner blended sheets, adds dots and stripes of contrast, and tops them with spritely polymer balls. The ink cartridges are removed during baking.

Cathy Barbaray, *Caliente Pendentif*; polymer; 2 inches (5cm). Photograph by the artist. Every trick in the polymer book is incorporated in Cathy's pendants. She unifies layers of patterns that include blends, canes, and colors with a stitched texture to achieve a look that is uniquely hers.

CHAPTER 2

Mixed Media

In contemporary craft, rare materials no longer make an object precious. In fact, mixed media artists delight in exploring new combinations of ordinary and unusual materials and techniques. Christine Damm embraces an eclectic mix of vintage and new materials; informed by years of working in textiles, pottery, and painting, she explores the conceptual blending of techniques and materials. Meanwhile, Claire Maunsell integrates her twenty years of glassblowing experience into polymer, discovering a new method that uses the clay's plasticity to form sinuous glasslike shapes.

The artists featured in this section are fueled by cross-disciplinary curiosity. You may be surprised where you find your own inspiration.

Opposite, clockwise from top:

Barbara Briggs, *Artifact Neck Piece*; polymer clay, bronze metal clay, and sterling silver; 16 inches (41cm). Photograph by the artist. Working in metals and semiprecious stones, Barbara, working from her Illinois studio, has gradually incorporated more polymer clay into her work.

Pat Bolgar, *Fringed Bracelet*; polymer, fine silver metal clay, and glass seed beads; 6 inches (15cm). Photograph by Jerry Anthony. This dense fringed bracelet showcases some of Pat's favorite materials. Growing up on a farm in Kansas, Pat learned the value of handcrafts at an early age.

Angie Wiggins, *Feathered Bowl*; polymer, feathers, paper, and glass; 8 x 10 x 10 inches (20 x 25.5cm). Photograph by the artist. Angie uses a variety of materials, including feathers, polymer, ball chain, and glass beads on a fanciful paper bowl. She learned embroidery at a young age and has been combining materials for years.

Liz Hall, *Mosaic Bangles*, *Tribal Series*; polymer, brass, and silver; 3 inch diameter (7.5cm). Photograph by the artist. Using "whatever shiny object catches [her] eye," Liz embeds mosaic chips of iridescent polymer opal and faux wood with black and white cane slices in brass bangle forms. Silver beads embedded in the black polymer grout add a dimensional touch.

Angie Wiggins, *Footed Paper Bowl*; polymer and paper; 4 x 6 inches in diameter (10 x 15cm). Photograph by the artist. Polymer legs add whimsy to the design of this paper bowl. Angie needed intense color that she couldn't find in other beads so she turned to polymer.

Marina Lombardi, *Dancing on the Lily Pads*; polymer and mixed media; 26 inches (66cm). Photograph by the artist. From her studio in Rome, Marina was inspired by the Art Nouveau style to create this focal bead, combined with hammered gilded wire, beads, semiprecious stones, pearls, antique brass elements, and metallic pigments.

Mareike Scharmer, *Fence Cap*; polymer over galvanized metal, 3½ x 3½ inches (9 x 9cm). Photograph by Rudolf Pollak. Mareike has covered lamps, mailboxes, furniture, and more with her fantastical home designs.

Angie Wiggins, *Footed Polymer Plate*; polymer, seed beads, and paint; 5 inches (12.5cm). Photograph by the artist. This footed square polymer plate combines cane slices with paints, textures, and seed beads.

Debra DeWolff, *Blue Mosaic Bangle*; polymer; 3 x 2½ inches (7.5 x 6.5cm). Photograph by Larry Sanders. The mosaics, made of embedded seed beads, appear through cutouts in the top layer of polymer.

Jon Anderson, *Tonero Mescalito*; 13 x 7 inches (33 x 18cm). Jon, who is long known for his polymer sculptures, also applies his polymer veneers to custom electric guitars and basses for Hand Guitars. He lives and works in Bali. This design is from his 2010 series. He produces 50-pound, 12-foot polymer canes for his large-scale production work.

Linda Ezerman, *Washed Ashore*; felt, polymer, resin, aluminum, rubber, miyki beads, thread, and ink; 18 inches (45.5cm). Photograph by the artist. Linda finds inspiration on the beaches of the Netherlands for her series entitled *Oh, That Southern Wind*.

Katrin Neumaier, *Faux Glass Earrings*; polymer, chalk, and sterling silver; 2 inches (5cm). Photograph by the artist. Katrin is a German artist who makes polymer look like glass in these earrings. The hollow aqua forms are made from translucent polymer that has been tinted with colored chalks. Bead caps and ear-wires are sterling silver.

Annie Pennington, *Diatom Series: Tucson Squiggle*, 2012; polymer, colored pencil, copper, and wool; 3 x 5 inches (7.5 x 12.5cm). Photograph by the artist. This piece was created as part of a staff challenge at *Art Jewelry* magazine, where Annie is an associate editor.

"I needed a process that's alive and fluid, like glass." —CLAIRE MAUNSELL

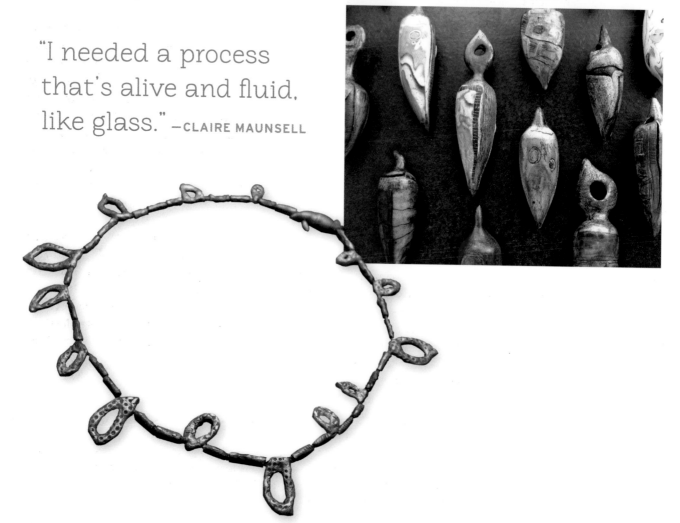

Claire Maunsell

Glass Roots ▸ Quebec, Canada

Claire Maunsell owes her polymer career to hot glass. "After attending the Sheridan College School of Crafts and Design, I was a professional glassblower for almost twenty years and ran a hot shop and gallery in Kingston, Ontario, for six of those years until children and job changes intervened," she says. When her husband joined the Canadian Navy in 2004, she sold all her glass equipment before their first posting. "It was a difficult turning point," admits Claire.

A maker of things all her life, Claire sought a new medium to explore between the demands of family life. Polymer was a natural choice. "I needed a process that's alive and fluid, like glass," she says. "As I started to design jewelry, I was initially drawn to this particular quality of polymer—and the fact that it is extremely lightweight compared to glass." As many have before her, Claire discovered that polymer shares working characteristics with hot glass, including its malleability, brilliant colors, and ability to reduce perfectly as millefiori canes. Though not consciously at first, she approached this new material with the experience and skill set developed by twenty years of working with hot glass. Two things she doesn't miss about glass? "Working in the studio through the summer and burning myself regularly."

Hot glass has informed Claire's work in unusual, cross-disciplinary ways. Years of creating hollow forms in glass and studying surface design have led to her current interest in applying those same techniques to polymer. Her current work features small, hollow polymer jewelry with lots of surface texture and color. In her glasswork, she created rich, layered surfaces of color using glass powders, canes, and shards built one upon the other. She brings that same layered style to polymer, drawing the viewer into an intimate relationship with the piece as she works with color in a

"detailed, painterly fashion." One of the biggest differences she notes between the two mediums is scale. "The challenge to perfect smaller work is very real for me!"

While at college studying glass, Claire encountered a design teacher who repeatedly preached the importance of *exhaustive* and *nonjudgmental* exploration of one's chosen material attempting a final design. "I thought he was a little crazy," laughs Claire. Twenty-five years later she understands the value of such exploration. "Ultimately," Claire says, "this is about jolting you out of complacency and making you realize that you *don't* know everything about your chosen medium—that, indeed, there is more to discover!" This important lesson taught her to pick up a piece of polymer and work with her hands when ideas lagged.

Through this exhaustive, nonjudgmental exploration, Claire has returned to her most essential motivation for working, what she calls "that still moment of creating and the intense satisfaction that momentarily accompanies it." Starting with simple, accessible techniques, she experiments endlessly and morphs basic shapes into complicated finished forms. "I don't do simple well," Claire says. She describes her polymer pieces as ancient-looking, often somber, and sometimes edgy.

Opposite, clockwise from top left:

Claire Maunsell in her studio in Gatineau, Quebec, near the magnificent Gatineau Park and close to the Canadian capital.

Pebble Box Chain Necklace; polymer; 17 inches (43cm). The beads are shaped so that they nestle against each other, hiding their connections but providing a flexible chain.

Claire has been working on a series of small hollow pod forms, bringing to polymer the skillset she developed working with glass.

Helena T Necklace; polymer and beads; 30 inches (76.2cm).

By focusing on her own journey of personal exploration, Claire is selective about finding inspiration among the bombardment of images available online. "We are all influenced—Pinterested, you might say!" admits Claire. She feels that the key to using such influences and finding her look is to honestly ask herself, "How does this work with what is in my head?" She has no qualms about discarding any techniques and forms that don't mesh well with those images. Focusing on her own experiments allows her to develop her own artistic vocabulary.

For Claire, this artistic vocabulary continues to be bilingual. "My apprenticeship with glass is helping to form me into the artist I'm becoming in polymer. My first love has prepared me for my second one."

By a Thread; polymer, acrylic, and copper wire; 17 inches (43cm). Claire fabricated this piece using glassmaking techniques—pulling, stretching, flaring, and constricting.

Clacker Claw Necklace; polymer; 28 inches (71cm).

Metallic Mosaic Pod Series; polymer and mixed media; 3 inches each (7.5cm). Claire layers image transfers, metallic paints, inks, and textures on prebaked forms. The layers build up complex and intriguing designs.

Project:
Lightweight Hollow Forms By Claire Maunsell

This technique is adapted for polymer from the techniques that Claire used for twenty years blowing glass. As many have previously discovered, the art of polymer millefiori has borrowed much from the world of glass. Polymer is also grand for making lightweight, hollow forms with a few very simple tools. These forms, once cured, can be a blank canvas to experiment with many color-application techniques. Let's take a look at round hollow forms, as they tend be the most troublesome shape to create.

TOOLS AND MATERIALS

well-conditioned polymer clay
  in white, 2 ounces (56g)

3 or more dowels in various
  diameters, from 1/8 inch (3mm)
  to 7/8 inch (2.2cm)

knitting needle or similar tool
  for smoothing

bowl of warm water, large enough
  to hold the bead

plastic resealable sandwich bag

skewer

X-Acto knife

needle tool for making vent holes
  in beads

scrap polymer and/or a light bulb,
  for molding the bead (optional)

baking soda and cornstarch

acrylic paints (optional)

texturing and/or carving tools
  (optional)

alcohol inks (optional)

INSTRUCTIONS

1. Take your well-conditioned ball of clay, roll it between your palms to compact it and create a uniform ball, and then flatten it slightly. With a ⅛-inch (3mm) or smaller dowel, make a hole in the center of the flattened ball, working the dowel through the clay from both ends of the ball. It is important to be precise from the beginning to maintain even walls.

2. Slide the flattened ball onto the dowel and gently roll the ball to make a fat tube. We need to make the tube longer and the walls thinner. Squeeze the sides of the tube, turn it 90 degrees, and squeeze again, making a square. Repeat this process on the corners of the square, making a rounded octagon. Gently roll to smooth it back to a round shape. If you roll from the start just using the dowels in the center, it is very easy to make uneven wall thicknesses. You can also roll lightly and stretch the polymer wider, alternating these two moves until the wall thickness is about ⅛ inch (3mm) or a little less. When learning this technique, leave the walls a bit thicker, as it will make the clay and the procedure more forgiving. Your first beads will be a bit heavier, but with practice, you can make quite amazingly thin-walled beads!

3. In this photo, you can see how the walls have been thinned down; there is now a lot of space around the dowel. Remove the first, smallest dowel and replace it with a larger one. While rolling these beads, use successively larger dowels so that they almost fill the space inside the tube. This way, you will avoid making grooves and thin areas.

TIP

I've used every type of clay commercially available, and, of course, they all have different characteristics. You can use any brand, but for this technique to work, the clay must be very well conditioned and soft. I often find that clay softener or liquid polymer must be mixed in well to improve the clay's ability to stretch. It might make the clay more loosey-goosey than you're used to, but trust me, it is necessary.

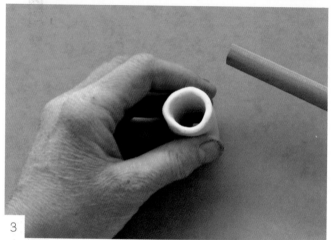

1

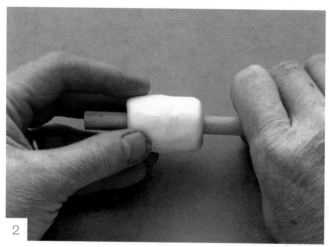

2

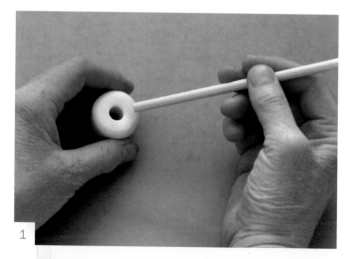

3

4 Here is the polymer tube on the larger dowel. Make sure that the walls are as thin and even as you'd like, because this is the last step before closing the ends. If you need to make the walls a little thinner, gently roll the larger dowel to enlarge the diameter of the hollow tube. Also make sure that the walls are even and that any surface imperfections have been gently smoothed away with a tool, such as a knitting needle.

5 In this photo, you can see that I am starting to constrict the opening. In order to help with closing the end, remove the large dowel and put in a slightly smaller one. Snug the dowel up to the inside and close the polymer against it. This helps avoid folds and creases, which are virtually impossible to remove. Keep scaling down the dowel until the hole is nearly closed. With practice, it can be done without dowels, but I recommend using them until you can constrict the opening evenly and neatly.

6 Neatly rolling and simultaneously constricting will produce a fine diameter of polymer that you can later pinch or slice off neatly.

7 As you finish the previous step, you'll notice that the end is rather bulbous, with a tail. Roll the end of the polymer tube on an angle to make a neat pencil point. In the glassmaking process, this technique is called *marvering*, and we'll be using it quite a lot from this point on to finish beads and to control the shape. Go a little easy on shaping the tube at this point because you have no air to resist your pressure.

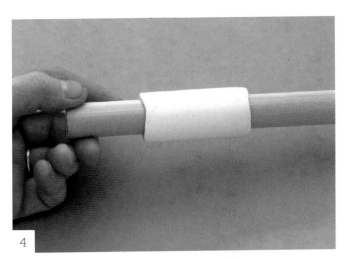

4

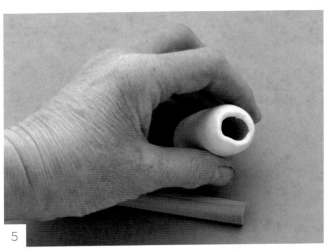

5

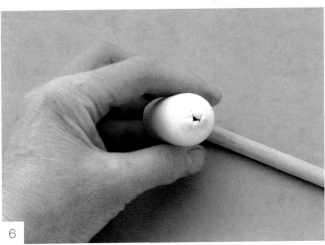

6

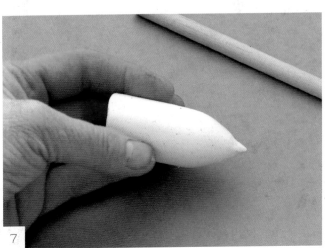

7

8 Turn your tube 180 degrees and begin to close the other end down, using successively decreasing sizes of dowel rods.

9 This photo shows the results of your efforts: a tube with one closed end and one with a small hole. Warm up the polymer slightly; the simplest way is to fill a bowl with warm to hot water and immerse the half-formed bead (inside a plastic sandwich bag) for 2–3 minutes.

Inflate the polymer tube with controlled, firm breaths, and seal up the end into which you have just blown. Then turn the tube 180 degrees, use a fine skewer to open up the end, and repeat the firm controlled inflation. Finally, reseal the end! Sounds simple, doesn't it?

And it is simple, except there are some potential pitfalls. If your walls are really thick, it will be difficult to inflate them. If your walls are really thin and your breaths particularly powerful, or if you have thin spots and uneven walls, it is easy to blow a hole right through the side. It's something you have to try and get a feel for. If you do blow out the side of your piece, do yourself a favor and scrap it. Start over and try blowing until you get the hang of it. It is virtually impossible to repair in a good way.

10 You can now easily roll the bead into the shape you want, since the air that's sealed inside the bead will resist your efforts. When you push on one area and move the wall inward, the air behind this area is forced to move elsewhere. Force the air into the middle belly of the bead to make the belly wider. Roll each end to move the pointed ends to the center of the bead.

11 Using an X-Acto knife, very carefully trim the points at either end. Use a knitting needle or a similar tool to smooth the scar.

12 The final step is to roll the roundish form between your palms into a true round shape. Go easy here; you don't want to crush your form or lose texture if you have it. If the clay is too soft to handle, let it cool for 10 minutes.

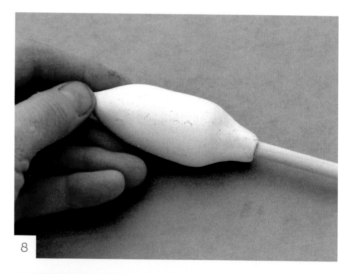

8

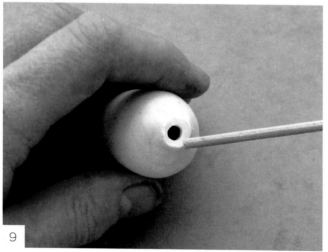

9

10

13 It is possible to capriciously decide to make your lovely globe into a lentil shape. I have created molds from scrap clay and light bulbs with different shapes to create a variety of smooth domes. Gently press your round into one of these to flatten it, flipping it often, smoothing, and paying particular attention to the edges.

14 Now you are ready to cure your work. First, be sure to make 1–2 small vent holes with the pin tool! This is important because sometimes the hollow forms will cave in or change shape without a vent hole, especially if there is a thin spot.

I use a 1:1 mixture of baking soda and cornstarch spread in an ovenproof dish to create a bed for the forms to lie on. Lay the pieces gently into preformed depressions in the bed. As the clay cures, regularly monitor the forms and turn them over periodically so that their exposure to the heat is uniform and they maintain their shape.

For fun, I finished my forms with color and carving. The textured round has a simple color wash of acrylic. The hollow form allowed me to keep lots of texture, something that is notoriously difficult to do while you are making solid texture forms.

I attacked the lentil bead with my Dremel carving tools, and then finished it with acrylic paint and alcohol inks.

Of course, there are dozens of other color and texture treatments that you could use on this form. It's just a canvas for you to explore a variety of techniques in polymer. And isn't that why we love this material?

11

12

13

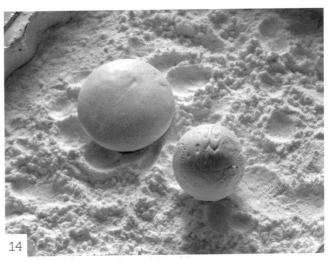

14

"I never met a texture I didn't like." —CHRISTINE DAMM

Christine Damm

Art Omnivore ► Vermont, United States

Christine Damm calls herself an art omnivore and considers herself a mixed media artist. "I look at everything and add what I like to the soup of ideas in my head," she says. Polymer allows her to work with color in 3-D and mix in other media and objects with abandon.

Many of Christine's influences come from her lifetime of travels and diverse artistic experiences, beginning with her childhood. Christine grew up in New Jersey and remembers traveling to New York City often to explore art. She got her first sewing machine at eight and started making doll clothes. In college she made her own clothes and sewed for other people. She entered the fashion world for a while. Then she bounced between four universities studying textiles, pottery, and painting before landing in 1977 in Berkeley, California, where she stayed for years, as an advisor to art history majors. In her fifties she decided she needed to settle down and get married. She moved East and bought a place with woods, streams, history, and farm animals. She checked out an online dating service, where she met her soul mate; they married in 2001.

She started with polymer by reading Tory Hughes's and Irene Dean's books. Entering *Art Bead Scene* blog challenges, writing articles for *Belle Armoire* magazine, and teaching at artBLISS events have helped her develop a body of polymer work and refine her style. Living in a rural area motivated her to reach out to other polymer artists and establish online connections, which led to new friendships with Claire Maunsell, Rebecca Watkins, and Genevieve Williamson, whose designs all share a sensibility with hers. They all like to work on the surface of the clay, applying materials and exploring as they go. They enjoy pushing the envelope and use mistakes as launch pads for better ideas.

Christine is drawn to small art adornments that have stories reflecting primitive themes. The tension between formal and tribal intrigues her, while shredded edges and dense layers appeal to her fascination with the dark side of the soul. The possibilities of metal clay with polymer have drawn her in that direction lately. When people complain that polymer clay isn't old or natural, she counters with "What's natural? It's from oil, and last I checked, that's from the earth." The old bones and found objects she mixes with polymer make her argument a convincing one. "It's that whole *wabi sabi* thing that I love. Let's destroy the surface a little bit," she says with a chuckle, "I never met a texture I didn't like."

As her work progressed, Julia Cameron's book *The Artist's Way* transformed Christine's way of looking at herself. She used to avoid calling herself an artist because she hadn't had any gallery shows. But *The Artist's Way* convinced her that since she thought like an artist, dressed like an artist, and lived like an artist, she was already an artist. Art made

---

Opposite, clockwise from top left:

Christine Damm in her studio in her 1830s home, which sits on thirty-four acres in rural Vermont.

Ming Earrings; polymer and mixed media; 2 inches (5cm). Polymer clay was added to vintage bracelet findings, colored with oil paint and gilders paste, and attached to handmade earwires.

Found Object Necklace; polymer and mixed media; 28 inches (71cm). A random collection of polymer beads and stones with some color affinity filled out the strand that ends in a polymer medallion topped with found objects.

Twisty Earrings; polymer and mixed media; 2 inches (5cm). The shape of exposed tree roots inspired Christine to wrap polymer strands around her finger, and add color with pencils and oils. Polished jasper rondelles add reflections.

her happy, and she claimed the title. Customers recognized her joy in her art. "You don't have to be torn up and edgy to be an artist," she reminds us. While most people approach problems, opportunities, and goals with the mind-set of "Have, Do, Be," Christine now subscribes to the "Be, Do, Have" theory. For example, most people think, "When I *have* a gallery show, then I will get to *do* more of the art I enjoy, and I will *be* more fulfilled." But Christine finds that her success has come when she reverses the order saying, "Starting right now, I will *be* more fulfilled, *do* more of the art that I enjoy, and then I will *have* the gallery show."

Storytelling is a theme throughout her work, so she calls her blog *Stories They Tell*. "I hear artists complain that they don't have a story to tell. I tell them that if they're alive, they have a story, but they may not be happy with it. So change it. Invent something new. Make it up. Remember what you enjoyed doing as a kid and get back there," she suggests. "You can go to a place that's wonderful with art. Producing art shouldn't be as painful as giving birth. It should be so intriguing that you don't want to leave. You can get in a bubble where everything else goes away—that's what I want people to experience when I teach. You can go to a wonderful, heavenly place and you don't have to die to get there. You can stay there as long as you want. This is as close to God as you're going to get because you've made something that never existed before. It's your connection to the universe. That's awe-inspiring to me, and it's the reason why I do art. I'm a maker, which is a very high position to be in. And we all have that potential."

Seedpod Earrings;
polymer clay, oil paint,
pencil; 2 inches (5cm).

Passion Flower Brooch; polymer clay and Whim-Z wire base; 3 inches (7.5cm). The beetle is all polymer with wire legs.

Kali Necklace; polymer clay and Whim-Z wire; 31 inches (79cm). The polymer clay pendant is formed using *mokume gane* (see page 69). The overlay is colored with pencil and embellished with twisted Whim-Z wire.

Project:
Sunshine and Clouds Layered Pendant By Christine Damm

Christine has always loved the pieced quilts called "sunshine and shadows," with their contrasting blocks of light and dark. She interprets a larger philosophical meaning in these designs—the idea that nothing in our world is exactly black or white, good or evil, night or day, but instead is more like a constantly shifting ground of illumination and cloudiness, inspiration and confusion, balance and excess, neither side prevailing but always dancing together. In this project, Christine illustrates a way of building shapes and layering colors that works with any jewelry element you want to design.

TOOLS AND MATERIALS

polymer clay (Premo! Sculpey) in white, beige, and translucent

sun motif

lightweight paper

pencil

scissors

pasta machine

disposable scalpel

clay-shaping tools

several different texture sheets

cornstarch (optional)

thin, round wire

craft gloves

needle tool

tissue blade

ball stylus in various sizes

brass round wire, 20-gauge, 4 inches (10cm)

chain-nose pliers

wire cutters

round-nose pliers

mold for the top piece

miscellaneous texture tools (buttons, molds, rubber stamps, etc.)

sponge cosmetic applicator

Thick Medium acrylic extender (Genesis)

acrylic craft paint in wasabi (yellow/green), sunshine yellow, light rust, dark turquoise, and slate blue

small, square paintbrushes

craft heat gun or toaster oven (optional)

400- to 600-grit wet/dry sandpaper

spray bottle for water

shallow tray for sanding

paper towels

heat-set oil paints (Genesis Oil Paints) in cadmium red, cadmium yellow pale, cadmium yellow deep, and alizarin crimson

Gilders Paste (Baroque Art) in cream and German silver

soft cloth

jump rings

beading wire

beads

chain

jewelry clasp

INSTRUCTIONS

1 Mix an ivory clay blend from Premo with 2 parts white to 1 part each of beige and translucent. Draw or copy a round sun motif, approximately 3 inches (7.5cm) in diameter, on a sheet of lightweight paper. Don't overthink it! The charm of this piece is that the rays are different sizes and textures. Cut the sun out with scissors. Roll out the beige/white/translucent mixture on a pasta machine at the medium-thick setting (5-6 playing cards) to a size that will accommodate your sun pattern. Press the cut-out pattern gently onto the clay so that it adheres firmly. With your scalpel, cut carefully around the pattern. Cut intersecting straight lines rather than trying to go around corners. Hold the blade as upright as possible to keep your edges straight.

2 Remove the paper pattern and refine the clay form with clay shapers to fix any distorted edges. Apply texture, using a different texture sheet for each segment. Take care not to overlap the textures or thin the edges too much. If your texture sheets are not silicone, be sure to use a release like cornstarch or water so your texture stamps won't stick to the clay. Define the segments by pressing a line between them using a thin, round length of wire.

3 Make another sheet of ivory clay just slightly larger than your main pattern and roll the clay out on the same setting as before. Put on the craft gloves and place the sun motif on top of the new slab of clay. Gently press the sun onto the new clay layer. Make sure you have good contact between the two, but don't smear or flatten the textured areas. Using a needle tool, draw cloud outlines lightly between the points of the segments.

4 Following the cloud lines you've drawn, cut out around the cloud shapes and the points of the segments with the scalpel. Slightly flatten the edges of the clouds with a clay-shaping tool and texture the edges,

1

2

3

4

making notches with a tissue blade and indents with a ball stylus.

5   Using a needle tool, make 2 holes through both layers of clay, about ⅝ inch (16mm) above the center of the top motif and ½ inch (13mm) to either side of the center. Smooth the holes with a clay shaper. Cure the piece at the manufacturer's suggested temperature for 30 minutes. Allow to cool.

6   Cut a 3-inch (7.5cm) piece of 20-gauge brass wire, and with the chain-nose pliers make two 90-degree bends in it, 1 inch (2.5cm) from each end. Insert the wire through the holes in the piece, from front to back.

7   With the wire cutters, trim the wires on the back of the piece to ¾ inch (2cm). Using the round-nose pliers, wrap each trimmed wire around the jaws of the pliers several times to form loops. Flatten these slightly to the side. These loops will provide attachments for jump rings and a chain so the piece can be strung as a pendant.

8   Continue building the center sun motif, adding 3 separate pieces. For the base, roll a ball of ivory clay ⅞ inch (2.2cm) in diameter and flatten it with your fingers into a disk about 1½ inches (3.8cm) in diameter and ⅛ inch (3mm) thick. This circle will need to be large enough to cover the attachment wire in the main motif and still be centered. For the middle disk, roll a second ball about 11/16 inch (18mm) in diameter—or about ¼ inch (6mm) smaller than the first—and press it onto the base disk. For the top piece, find an interesting motif from a mold, either purchased or handmade. (I used an antique button.) Roll a ball of clay 7/16 inch (11mm) in diameter and press it into the mold. It should be about the right size for the top layer of the center stack. Leave the edges uneven and press it onto the top of the stack. Use texture tools to refine all the clay layers.

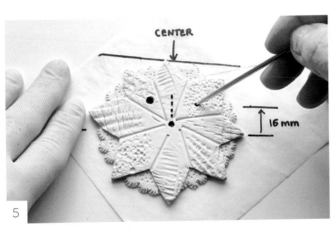

5

6

7

8

9 Using a cosmetic sponge applicator, scoop out a ¼-inch (6mm) ball of acrylic medium and smear it carefully all over the bottom of the uncured center sun-motif stack. Apply it thicker in the middle of the stack, as it will be forced out to the edges when you press the two pieces together. Using gloved hands, place the center sun motif on top of the larger, already-cured piece and press gently but firmly all over the motif to ensure good contact between the two. Cure the entire piece for 1 hour at the manufacturer's suggested temperature.

10 Apply color as follows: Lay down a base of wasabi (yellow/green) acrylic paint on the textured sun's rays and on the outer ring of the center sun motif base, using a small, square paintbrush to get the paint into the texture. Apply sunshine yellow acrylic to the center motif in the same way. Dab the light rust acrylic into the dotted depressions. Allow the paint to dry and cure by heating with a craft heat gun or in the oven for 15 minutes.

11 Using 400- to 600-grit wet/dry sandpaper, a spray bottle of water, and a shallow tray, sand off some of the paint so there's space for the next color. Using the square paintbrush again, pick up a small amount of dark turquoise paint and dab the excess onto a paper towel so that the brush is almost dry. Lightly layer the dark turquoise paint over the light green, sweeping the paint onto the sanded areas.

9

10

11

NOTE

This technique of applying color is a process of painting, curing, and sanding, clearing off the high points of the texture so they can accept a new color of paint. It's addition and subtraction, not mixing, and produces a unique effect. If you don't like what you've painted in any step, simply sand it off and do it over.

12 Paint the cloud shapes with the slate blue acrylic. Lightly dab on a layer of slate blue acrylic to the base of the sun's rays with an almost-dry, small paintbrush. Allow the paint to dry, then cure as you did with the previous color and lightly sand the cloud edges.

13 Using the heat-set oil paints, mix a red-orange color using cadmium red and cadmium yellow pale. Using your little finger, dab small amounts of this color on the outside edges of the sun's rays and the center motif and rub it in. Rub small amounts of cadmium yellow deep oil paint on the edges of the clouds. Cure again. Sand the edges of the sun's rays and the center motif. Using a small amount of alizarin crimson blended with some red-orange paint, dab a small amount on the edges to make them pop. Dab the

reverse side of the piece all over with the slate blue acrylic using your little finger. Cure the entire piece one final time for 15 minutes at the manufacturer's suggested temperature.

14 Apply the cream Gilders Paste with a paintbrush very lightly—just a frosting—to the inside edge of the sun's rays and the base of the clouds. Then apply the German silver Gilders Paste lightly over the high points of the entire piece with your little finger. Allow to dry for 12 hours and buff with a soft cloth.

15 To finish as a pendant, attach jump rings to the loops on the back of the pendant. Attach beading wire to the jump rings and string on beads and a chain. Complete with a clasp.

12

13

14

15

CHAPTER 3

Textures

Here are artists who texture, stamp, carve, paint, and polish polymer into something else, defying the old notion that polymer can look a little, well, plastic. Natalia García de Leániz stamps ordinary materials into the clay to break up the surface and make the tactile experience of her beads as appealing as her bright palette. Genevieve Williamson sands, carves, and paints her muted pieces for a more primitive and rough-hewn look.

Artwork in the gallery that follows will have you wondering, "Is it glass? Metal? Fabric?" Textures add that extra allure to fool the eye.

Opposite, clockwise from top left:

Linda Ezerman, *Necklace*; polymer, glass beads, and copper; 24 inches (61cm). What look like pieces of rock and bone are actually polymer from this Dutch artist's *Beachcombing* series.

Barbara Fajardo, *Art Nouveau Earrings*; polymer; 2 inches (5cm). Photograph by the artist. This three-dimensional textured design by a New Mexico-based artist was achieved with the Sutton Slice method similar to the sprigging technique used to embellish Wedgewood china.

Maria Belkomor, *Twisted Bracelet*; polymer and brass; 3 inch diameter (7.5cm). Photograph by the artist. Maria, a Russian artist, extrudes strings of polymer, positions the strings around a solid color core, and gently twists to spiral the colors and add texture. The ends are finished here with brass bead caps.

Donna Greenberg, *Rivers of Vulcan*; polymer, iron pyriate, bronze, and brass; 3 inches wide (7.5cm). Photograph by the artist. This trio of cuffs made with black and metallic clay was inspired by the colors and textures of volcanic activity. The surface of the clay is deeply impressed to appear rough.

Janice Abarbanel, *Rainforest Necklace*; polymer, stainless steel cable, and sterling silver; 16 inches (41cm). Photograph by the artist. Janice was inspired by a vacation zip line ride through the forest in Belize. Flecks of metallics, crackled surfaces, and organic shapes add texture.

Page McNall, *Weathered Chevron Shield Necklace*; polymer and mixed media; 2 inches (5cm). Photograph by the artist. Using thin layers of colors backed by black (the "watercolor technique"), Page covered the pendant, baked the piece, and then scratched the surface to distress it. The scratches were accented with black acrylic paint. The pendant is accented with ceramic and glass beads and brass elements.

Rebecca Geoffrey, *Layered Designs*; polymer, 1½ inch beads (3.8cm). Photograph by the artist. Rebecca, a Canadian artist, adds texture to this pile of beads by neatly cutting designs out of one layer of polymer and applying it over a contrasting layer of color.

Rebecca Geoffrey, *Carved Pendants*; polymer and sterling silver, 1½ inches each (3.8cm). Photograph by the artist. More recently, Rebecca creates texture by carving her designs into polymer. She accents the carving with paint and sets the polymer in her own hand fabricated sterling silver bezels.

Libby Mills, *Scribbled Beads*; hollow 1-inch polymer beads with wire beads on rubber cord. Photograph by Cynthia Tinapple. Libby scratched designs on these beads and drew on them with colored pencils.

Eva Thissen, *Sakura Earrings*; polymer, brass, grossular garnet rondelles, glass beads, and gold-filled findings. Tiny bits of polymer are appliquéd onto a polymer base to achieve a textured image on these earrings, which are based on cherry blossoms.

Helen Breil, *Waterfall*; polymer clay, rubber cording, and glass beads; 4 x 3 inches (10 x 7.5cm). Photograph by the artist. A founding member of the Southern Ontario Polymer Clay Guild, Helen twists polymer into unusual shapes and adds texture and interest by stamping its surface.

Lynda C. Moseley, *Faux Jade Asian Kanji Focal Beads*; 2 x ¾ inches (5 x 2cm). Photograph by the artist. The subtle texture of tinted translucent clay is accentuated by buffing the raised designs.

Tanya Mayorova, *Spiral Layered Bangle*; polymer; 2 inches wide (5cm). Photograph by the artist. Tanya, from Russia, applies slices of extruded cane with layer overlapping colorful layer to create a bangle that is rough with texture and rich with texture. The design circles around one small stone.

Silvia Ortiz de la Torre, *Nidos Bracelet*; polymer; 3 inch diameter (7.5cm). Photograph by the artist. Five polymer circles are linked to each other with neoprene cord, the ends of which have been glued into polymer balls. The piece stretches onto the wearer's wrist, while the riot of color and unusual construction provide texture.

"Experimenting is necessary." —NATALIA GARCÍA DE LEÁNIZ

Natalia García de Leániz

Transmitting Happiness ▸ Madrid, Spain

W hile on vacation a few years ago, Natalia García de Leániz bought several packages of polymer in a craft shop in London. When she returned home to Madrid, she was hooked. Natalia had grown up active and creative and studied advertising and graphic design in school. "I had a job in advertising, but I don't know how to be without making. This is what I need," she says. When she would arrive home tired and worn out from the office, what she needed was not rest or food: She needed to make something. Natalia keeps a big supply of ideas in her head as well as notebooks full of drawings and folders of magazine cutouts. "When something comes to me, I have to make it right away. It all comes together, and the connections get made," she says.

As her interest in polymer grew, Natalia returned to the United Kingdom for the British Polymer Clay Guild's annual retreat, where she met Alison Gallant, Carol Blackburn, and other artists. "I want this in my country," she thought, and she set out to create a forum where she could share her newfound passion. She located polymer enthusiasts in Spain on an Internet forum, and in 2006, she started the Asociación Arcilla Polimérica de España (Spanish Polymer Clay Association) with the handful of polymer artists that she knew. The guild grew to 250 members, mostly young people. "They are like sponges, soaking up everything. Polymer is much newer here than in the United States," she explains.

Natalia had set up a shop in Madrid to sell supplies but closed it when the economy worsened and as polymer became increasingly more available in Spain than it was even a few years prior. Now, she and her husband, Dani, both experiment with polymer and have traveled to the United States to teach several times. Though they share a design sense and think alike, they work very differently. She explains that, for her, "Experimenting is necessary. I don't like following rules and steps. It's how my mind works. I am a bit of a mess when I'm working." Painstaking research and long, detailed instructions aren't her methodology. "I get bored if I have fifty steps to follow." She's not in pursuit of the perfect result and finds that she must enjoy what she does. "My husband is completely the opposite," she adds. "He thinks like an engineer—logical, patient, methodical." The two find that their approaches—one spontaneous and the other analytical—allow them to think differently and balance each other.

Since Natalia was diagnosed with multiple sclerosis in 2007, the hardest part of her journey through setbacks and treatments has been when she's told to do nothing. "Doing nothing is horrible; it's the worst thing. Some days my mind thinks one thing but my hands won't do it. So during the last bad time I made one bead a day. Just one bead. I've kept that necklace. It's a treasure for me."

Opposite, clockwise from top left:

Natalia García de Leániz in her studio in Madrid.

Textured Mokume Earrings; polymer; 1½ inches (3.8cm). Natalia uses a small piece of air filter material to texture the base bead and adds colored shapes by using her streamlined *mokume gane* technique.

Funky Desert Bracelets; polymer; 3 inch diameter (7.5cm). Prebaked crumbles of polymer are pressed into the textured clay to provide even more relief on these funky creations.

Bumpy Bangles; polymer; 3 inch diameter (7.5cm). Black beads with colorful spots are interspersed between rough flat beads in a variation of Natalia's project (see page 69).

When Natalia had her own shop, she didn't like to sell her own pieces and still doesn't wear what she makes. "When I make a piece, I love it, and then I'm done with it," she says. Although she is shy about her own work, she loves to wear polymer from friends like Donna Kato, Judy Belcher, Dan Cormier, Grant Diffendaffer, Sarah Shriver, Leslie Blackford, Lindly Haunani, Jana Roberts Benzon, and others she's persuaded to come to teach in Spain. "Those pieces represent friends, stories, love," she explains.

Natalia's friends and family are eager to wear her work, and she feels great when something she's created inspires or moves someone else. Through the use of vibrant colors and whimsical patterns, Natalia aims to "transmit happiness" through her work. "I'm a happy person, and I have to make what I'm feeling," she adds matter-of-factly. Her life, her relationships, and her art have taught her that she has many great blessings in life. "We have to appreciate those things every day," she says. "Every day."

Flat Black Bead Necklace; polymer on 24-inch cord. The base beads are heavily textured before slices of cane and bits of metallic clays are added to the edges.

Natalia and her husband, Daniel Torres Mancera, collaborated on this thin hollow *Radiolarian* bracelet series. Kato Polyclay gives these fragile designs their strength.

Chunky Bracelet; polymer; 3 inch diameter (7.5cm). Natalia cut striped stacks of polymer into beads and textured the top surface. Holes reveal the patterns below and polymer balls are set in the recesses.

Wobbling Mokume Bracelet
By Natalia García de Leániz

Natalia's project is based on traditional *mokume gane*, an ancient Japanese art using layered metal. Most of the polymer variations of this technique involve shaving the surface of a stack of multicolored layers of clay. In Natalia's method, the shaved bits and pieces actually become the design elements. This technique allows for more control over the results and requires a thinner stack of colors. The colors pop off the black background, creating a modern version of this ancient craft. Best of all? It's easy.

TOOLS AND MATERIALS

polymer clay in black and
    4 contrasting colors of your choice
pasta machine
thin knitting needle (3-4mm)
tissue blade
black wire, 20- to 22-gauge
wire cutters
jewelry pliers
acrylic roller
ball stylus embossing tool, drinking
    straws, and/or pen caps
elastic cord, 7-8 inches long

INSTRUCTIONS

1 Roll a sheet of black clay at a medium thickness (3-4 playing cards) through your pasta machine, wrap it around a thin knitting needle, and roll it with your hands until no seams are visible. Bake it for 25 minutes at the temperature recommended by the manufacturer.

2 While it is still warm, remove the clay from the needle. You will have a cylinder with a hole in the middle.

3 Cut the cylinder into ¼- to ½-inch (6 to 13mm) pieces. These will be your small black beads for making the bracelet. You will need a total of 6-7 inches (15-18cm) of these tube beads.

4 Make 12-15 round black balls ¾ inch (2cm) in diameter and press them a little bit with your fingers toward your work surface so they each have one flat area.

1

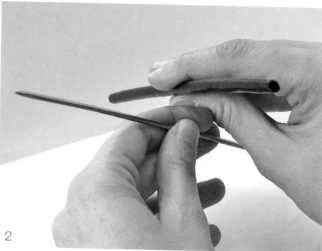

2

3

4

5 Cut 12-15 pieces of 20- to 22-gauge black wire, each 1½ inches (4cm) long. Curve one end, and insert the curved end into the flat side of the balls. (The curve captures the wire in the clay so that you can't pull it out.) Use a knitting needle or other sculpting tool to roll the flat clay a bit, making sure the wire is well embedded and trapped inside it. Bake the pieces for 30 minutes. Do not bend the wire until the piece has cooled.

6 Using jewelry pliers, form a loop and wrap the wire several times around the base of the loop. Trim the excess wire with wire cutters and flatten the wire end.

7 Roll 4 sheets of different, contrasting colors of clay through the pasta machine on a medium-thick setting (5-6 playing cards) and stack them.

8 With the acrylic roller, compact the block more and make it a bit thinner. Pass the 4-layer sheet through the thick setting (7-8 playing cards) of your pasta machine.

5

6

7

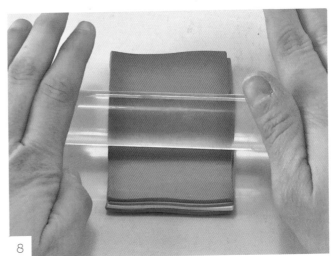

8

9 Cut the sheet in half with the tissue blade and stack these two halves.

10 Repeat steps 8 and 9. You will have now a sheet with 16 layers.

11 Using objects like drinking straws, pen caps, and ball-stylus tools, make impressions in the clay stack. Make deep indentations but do not go all the way through the clay.

12 Shave off pieces of clay by bending your tissue blade and slicing off the tops of the indentations. Place these clay chips aside as you shave your sheet. If you need more bits, you may be able to flip the stack over, make some indentations with your tools and shave more pieces from the bottom of the stack.

9

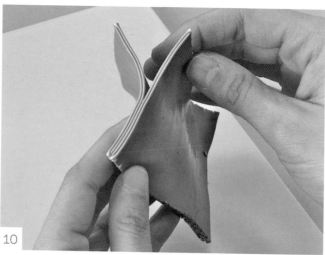

10

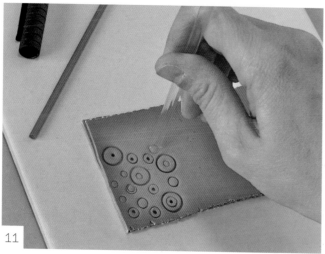

11

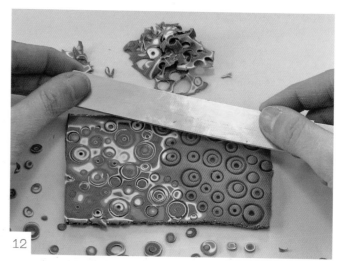

12

13 Arrange the clay chips on the black balls, leaving space between the chips. Arrange them lightly until you are pleased with their placement. When you are satisfied, push them onto the surface of the beads more securely. Bake the beads again.

14 String 2–4 small tubular beads between each of the big mokume ones onto an elastic cord and knot the ends together. Hide the knot by pulling it back into one of the tube-bead holes.

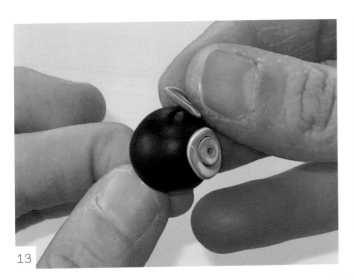
13

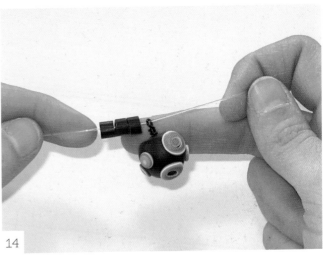
14

Make several of these bracelets for an even more dynamic look.

"Exploration
is infectious."

—GENEVIEVE WILLIAMSON

Genevieve Williamson

Play Is the Essence ▸ Pennsylvania, United States

Genevieve Williamson is a mother, artist, and wife who lives in a tiny rural Pennsylvania town. Her family shares a 120-year-old home with her parents, and she homeschools her three children. But you'd be wrong if you pictured Genevieve as a little-house-on-the-prairie kind of girl. She spends a portion of almost every day in her attic studio creating sophisticated rough-hewn polymer art.

In 2007 Genevieve's husband was given all the supplies and equipment for setting up a polymer studio. He brought them home and asked her if she'd like to play with it. "You're unhappy when you're not making," her husband reminded her.

"The box sat there for weeks and eventually I gave in. I looked up information online and found *Polymer Clay Daily*. I saw people doing all kinds of things and realized this is a legitimate material," she discovered. "Polymer is approachable. In other mediums, where would you be after two hours of instruction, let alone just reading? Two hours of watercolor? Two hours on a spinning wheel or at a loom? But you can really get started in polymer after just two hours."

Art has always been part of everyday life for Genevieve. Her mother quilts, her father is a retired high school art teacher, and Genevieve's husband is a photographer and painter who teaches high school art. As central as art was to her growing up, it wasn't pushed, but she was allowed to explore and given whatever materials she was interested in. In kindergarten she was surprised to find that not everyone made their own cards, wrapping paper, and fabrics like they did in her home. Genevieve started college as a graphic design major. As she pictured her future, she realized she didn't want the life of a graphic designer. The college

sculpture department was full so Genevieve chose crafts, with a concentration in metal, a study of crafts that made her particularly interested in how art is constructed.

The issues raised in her metalwork are just as relevant to her exploration of polymer today. "How do I construct things?" she asks. "How strong is polymer clay? What can I get polymer to do? Exploration is infectious." Though she was trained in metals, Genevieve envisions metals taking a supportive role in her art. She'd like to make her own findings in order to completely control the design of her pieces. "I like large pieces that each make a statement and stand on their own, so as I become more confident I hope my pieces will become larger and more complex. I designed at the bench when I worked in metal, and to some degree I do the same with polymer. I draw vague sketches with no texture, no color, just shapes. I make mock-ups. I wait for something to happen. It's an organic approach."

Genevieve doesn't know polymer artists in her area, and the closest guild is an hour away, in Harrisburg. "While the Pennsylvania Guild of Craftsmen has been supportive, I'd be stuck if it weren't for online connections. That's my community. I reconnected with Lynn Lunger when we ran into each other on Etsy; we went to college together. I met Claire Maunsell through *Polymer Clay Daily*, and we clicked

---

Opposite, clockwise from top left:

Genevieve Williamson retreats to the quiet of a third-floor studio in her Pennsylvania home.

Buoy Necklace; polymer; 18 inches (45.5cm). Each bead is formed over a lightweight core and carved and distressed after curing.

South Atlantic Pin; polymer; 2 inches long (5cm). This is the first in Genevieve's *Landscape/ Seascape* series.

Mix Drop Earrings; polymer and oxidized sterling silver; 2 x ½ inches (5 x 3.8cm). A mix of modern shape with rustic texture, these gray earrings are carved both before and after curing.

right away." With two sons at home, Genevieve finds that the website Etsy works well as her sales venue. She opened her online shop in 2008, and it gave her easy access to an interested audience. Several galleries as well as individual collectors found her on Etsy and began acquiring her work. With her commitment to homeschooling, Genevieve doesn't have the time to produce the quantity of work required for big shows. But a recent surge in attention and acclaim has made her look ahead and prepare for a bigger commitment, even if it does feel a long way off.

As her art gains attention, Genevieve is more aware of an ongoing inner struggle. As she works, cautionary critics in her head start nagging, asking, "How much should I charge? How much time have I put into this? How do I balance life and work?" She explains that "Some voices are my own, some are other people's, and some are cultural."

Genevieve stops the back-and-forth critical conversation in her head saying, "Play is my job—I try to remember that." She even talks fondly about her imaginary friends from her childhood, Jibby and Juna, who still act as her muses. "Play is the essence. If I lose that idea, then the life of a piece gets lost. Imagination is a child's language. So is art. I'm not answering any big questions or curing diseases. I'm just dealing with thoughts, hopes, fears, memories, all in the language of childhood. So I know I have to keep my receipts and pay my taxes, but I can't forget to let myself play."

Sediment 1 Bracelet; polymer; 3 inch diameter (7.5cm). Subtle layers of color circle the wearer's wrist in flat layered beads that look like sedimentary rocks.

Genevieve lines up some variations on her project earrings (opposite page). Shape, size, and color can be varied to suit your own preferences.

Carved Bead Bracelet; polymer, glass, and leather; 6 inches long (15cm). Carved, pierced, distressed, and faux bone polymer beads are linked by matte, glass beads on leather cord.

Project:
Variations on a Theme Earrings

By Genevieve Williamson

These three-in-one earrings give the wearer delightful options. The drops that dangle beneath the dark dishes can be turned to either side: You decide whether you want to show off the bright or neutral color. A metalsmith by training, Genevieve embeds her ear wires in polymer and bends them to allow for switching components. She textures the clay in thoughtful and inventive ways that give the clay a rough and raw appeal.

TOOLS AND MATERIALS

small balls of conditioned polymer clay in white, gray, and turquoise

smooth work surface

pasta machine

round cutter (Kemper); sample is ¾ inch (2cm) in diameter

glass pebbles (used in flower arranging)

release agent, such as cornstarch

acrylic roller

tissue blade (Kemper)

card stock and pencil (optional)

scrap clay (optional)

texturing tool

large needle

sterling silver wire, 20-gauge

wire cutters

pliers

heavy pin, utility knife, or small carving tool

cyanoacrylate glue

wet/dry sandpaper (or use regular sandpaper with a face mask)

black acrylic paint

small paintbrush

paper towels

steel wool

wire rounder or needle-nose file

piece of denim for polishing

plastic earring backs (optional)

INSTRUCTIONS

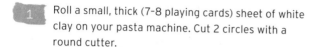

1 Roll a small, thick (7-8 playing cards) sheet of white clay on your pasta machine. Cut 2 circles with a round cutter.

2 Tap the rounded side of your glass pebbles with a powdery release agent such as cornstarch. You want a thin covering—not too much but not so little that you can't see it on the glass. This is what makes the pitted yet slightly shiny texture in the concave portion of the disk.

3 Press the circles onto the glass pebbles as close to center as possible. The clay won't want to stick at first but gently press with your pointer finger on the top and your thumb on the bottom, turning the disk as you go. Eventually the clay will yield and fit snugly to the pebble. Set aside.

4 Roll the gray clay to a thickness of 7-8 playing cards on your pasta machine. Roll the turquoise clay to a thickness of 3-4 playing cards and place on top of the gray. Cut out a 3 × 3-inch (7.5 × 7.5cm) square. Gently roll over it with an acrylic roller to join the colors. Bend your tissue blade and use it to cut the curved sides of 2 wing shapes. If you are uncomfortable cutting freehand, draw a wing-shaped pattern on card stock. I look for balanced shapes rather than mirror images so I prefer the freehand approach. You can practice cutting on some scrap clay beforehand if you are unsure of yourself.

5 Add texture to the turquoise side of the clay. I wanted a texture that would create a visual contrast to the disk, so I used my blade to make vertical lines in the turquoise clay. Don't cut too deeply.

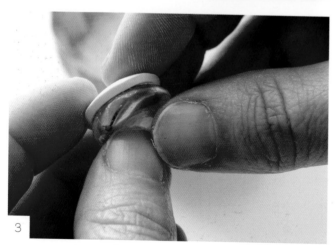

1

2

3

4

6 Using a needle, make a hole for the wire to go through. Put it in the center of the turquoise piece, about 3/16 inch (5mm) from the top. Bake all the pieces according to the manufacturer's instructions and allow them to cool. While the pieces are baking, cut two 2 1/4-inch (5.5cm) pieces of 20-gauge sterling silver wire. Using pliers, bend a 1/4-inch (6mm) section at the end of each.

7 When the polymer clay pieces are cool, carve a notch into the back of each white disk. This is easiest to do with the disks still attached to the pebbles for support. Using a heavy pin, utility knife, or other small carving tool, start just above the center and carve to within 1/8 inch (3mm) of the edge of the disk. Be careful to only carve as deep as your sterling silver wire is thick. I suggest carving just a bit and then checking to see

if the bent section of the wire fits, then carving more if necessary. A snug fit is best. Using a small dot of cyanoacrylate glue, attach the wire to the disk. The glue holds the wire in place while you complete the next step. Allow the glue to dry completely.

8 Using a small amount of very soft white clay, cover the glued wire completely. Spread the clay from the center to the outside of the disk while smoothly tapping and "healing" the clay. Add more clay if needed to cover the wire completely. You will sand the area later, but careful work now saves you from having too much finishing work to do. Take your time to make sure the wire is snugly embedded. Rebake the disks and allow them to cool. Take the disks off the pebbles.

5

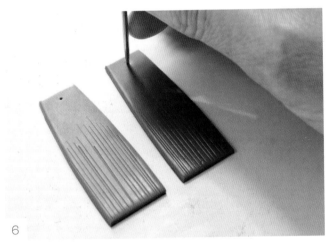

6

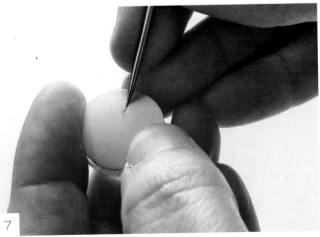

7

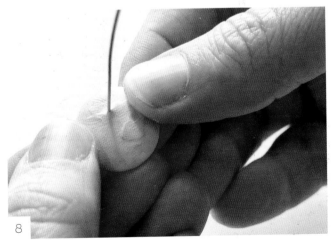

8

9 Sand the edges of the wing pieces to create slightly rounded corners. You can use the highest grit of wet/dry sandpaper under running water or, wearing a mask, use standard sandpaper. Sand the gray side of the wing in both directions to create texture. Darken the wing pieces and white disks with black acrylic paint and wipe away excess immediately with a paper towel. Remove even more of the paint with steel wool to further enhance the textures. You may want to repeat this process of painting and removing several times to get a finish you like, but remember that the pieces will get darker as you go. The sample earrings were painted two times.

10 I like to remove almost all the black from the very rims of the white disks to accentuate the circular shape. To create a matte finish, heat-set the acrylic by putting the pieces back in the oven for about 15 minutes.

11 When the polymer has cooled, create a bend in the sterling silver wire about as wide as the thickest part of your pliers. You want the bend to be thick enough to go through your ear with the addition of the wing but not so thick that when you are wearing just the inverted disk it doesn't move around.

12 For comfort, round the end of the sterling silver with a file. Polish the wing lightly with a piece of denim. Attach the wing to the disk by sliding it up the wire and swiveling it around as it goes around the bend. Because the earrings are so lightweight, it's best to wear them with clear plastic earring backs to ensure that they don't slip out.

9

10

11

12

Online Outreach

When Canadian artists Dan Cormier and Tracy Holmes offered their book *Relief Beyond Belief: Silhouette Dieforming in Polymer Clay* as a downloadable e-book, they were amazed at how far their lessons would spread. Dan, a well-traveled teacher, recalls the book's journey around the world. "Our *Relief Beyond Belief* book was written in Mexico, and has been downloaded by students in more than thirty countries so far. When I was selling my Fimo beads from a blanket in Montreal twenty years ago, I never would have guessed how far polymer would travel."

Dan Cormier, *Master Class Necklace*; polymer; 27 inches (69cm). Photograph by the artist. This study in polymer silhouette die-forming was featured in Dan's *Relief Beyond Belief* e-book. He has become known for his refined and thoroughly researched methods, in stark contrast to the early beads that he sold on the streets in Montreal.

CHAPTER 4

Characters

Monsters, manga, heroes, and fairies—all these characters can come alive in polymer. Camille Young, an American artist, points to Japanese manga and anime artists who heavily influenced her sculpted figures, as well as computer games where characters are trapped in a two-dimensional world. In the gallery you'll find other artists from a number of countries whose fanciful characters express quirky views, twists of nature, fantasy worlds, or dark thoughts. Polymer allows artists to render these imaginary creatures from other worlds to the point where they can seem quite real.

Opposite, clockwise from top left:

Jacky Mullen, *Small Snail Sculpture*; polymer; 4 inches tall (10cm). Photograph by the artist. Jacky sculpts the spirits of the glen that she imagines around her home in Scotland.

Jacky Mullen, *A Handful of Pistachios*; polymer and pistachio nut shells; each less than an inch high. Jacky finds her characters in the most unlikely places!

Cat Hamlin, *Luna—Black Lab Memorial*; polymer with metallic inclusions; 3 x 1 inches (7.5 x 2.5cm). Photograph by the artist. This Czech artist's subtly sculpted polymer convinces us that this black Lab continues to wait patiently for her master's attention.

Elena Samsonova, *Salty Little Creatures*; polymer cured on square glass salt and pepper shakers with detachable tops; 1 x 2 inches tall (2.5 x 5cm). Designed by a Brooklyn-based Russian artist, the heads of these characters can be twisted off and interchanged.

Edgar Hernandez, *Vita Lectiones*, 2012; polymer clay, acrylic paint, wood, fabric, and buttons; 22 x 13 x 4 inches (56 x 33 x 10cm). Photograph by the artist. In each of his pieces, Edgar's red-nosed melancholy character accentuates lost, lonely feelings that the viewer can sympathize with.

Nicole Johnson, *Snowmen Under Attack*; polymer and acrylic paint; 7 inches tall (18cm). Photograph by the artist. Nicole's characters are mostly grumpy misfits with issues and have a certain charm about them.

Doreen Kassel, *Missus Piggy Music Box*; polymer and music box; 3 inch diameter (7.5cm). Photograph by the artist. Part of Doreen's *Whimsical Music Box* series, this character plays "You Are My Sunshine."

Nicole Johnson, *Bob*; polymer and acrylic paint; 7 inches tall (18 cm). Photograph by the artist. Nicole identifies herself as a monster maker.

Leslie Blackford, *Tinapple Shrine* and characters from the Tinapple collection; 6 inches tall (15cm). Photograph by Cynthia Tinapple. Leslie created this polymer shrine in 2007 and the characters—individually titled *Snakes Nest*, *Lion King*, *Circus Bear*, and *Briefcase Bear*—were spontaneously created at polymer events the two artists attended together.

Selena Anne Wells, *Armless Goddess*; Cernit clay; 4½ inches (11cm). Photograph by the artist. Selena's textured and distressed characters, such as this faux ivory sculpture, have an archaeological air about them.

Sophie Skein, *Deer Wedding Cake Topper*; polymer with glass eyes; 4 inches tall (10cm). Photograph by the artist. Mule deer, indigenous to western North America, are graceful animals with dreamy eyes, large ears, cloven hooves, and white tails with black tips. The young buck has forked antlers and sports a glass flower boutonniere. The doe wears a flower behind her ear.

Mike Leavitt, *Art Army Banksy*; polymer clay, Styrofoam, and steel armatures; 10 inches tall (25.5cm). Photograph by the artist. This articulated figure of the famous graffiti artist is poseable with moving arms, head, and legs.

543_r4
279 ppi

"When I combined my love of video games and art I knew I'd found my perfect niche." —CAMILLE YOUNG

Camille Young
Video Game–Inspired Art ➤ Arizona, United States

Camille first wanted to be a sculptor in 1985 when she was four, and she still remembers the piece that sparked her interest in polymer and character-based sculpture. Her mother was in an art group, and one of the group members showed Camille a beautiful little foal that she had formed out of Sculpey. It looked perfect to Camille's four-year-old eyes. She was instantly inspired and wanted to try it herself. Her mother generously shared her art supplies and gave her daughter lots of encouragement. "My first piece was a green Sculpey dragon that had gold spikes running down its back, and I was very proud to be an artist," she recalls.

Camille grew up surrounded by video games, but instead of playing *EarthBound, Super Mario RPG,* and *The Legend of Zelda: Ocarina of Time* with her brother, she would sculpt polymer with them as her inspiration. The art in the video games drew her in and she developed a great appreciation for the aesthetics of these virtual worlds. She acknowledges that "video games definitely brought my brother and me closer, and in the process, games became my muse."

One of the few games Camille and her brother played together was *Mario Paint,* which included a special mouse controller for making drawings, animations, and music with any TV. The concept was thrilling to her. "When I saw the clay models pictured in the guide that came with the game *EarthBound,* I was fascinated by how artist Masao Tottori had translated the villains and heroes from pixilated game sprites into sculpted figures," she says. Camille realized that the clay versions gave the game an entirely new dimension that the two-dimensional artwork simply couldn't capture.

Her brother suggested that Camille submit her game-inspired art to a website for *EarthBound* fans in April of 1999. They posted her art on the popular website Starmen.net, which she checked every day to marvel that her creations were on display. Camille continued to submit her pieces and hang around the site, which led her to meet her husband in the forums. They married in 2004 as her husband was finishing his computer graphics technology degree, and they dreamed of starting an online business together.

Camille had graduated with a degree in fine art from Pima Community College in 2002 and worked at a small local cookie business where she decorated, baked, and helped customers. "But that didn't leave me with much time or energy for art at the end of the work day," she says. "I felt depleted and run-down when I wasn't creating." Though she relied on the job and appreciated the work, she left in July 2007 after much thought and prayer. She knew she needed to take her art more seriously. Neglecting her creative side for several years made it difficult to get back in the habit,

Opposite, clockwise from top left:

Camille Young in her Arizona-based studio.

Turtle; polymer; 2 inches (5cm). This faux ceramic turtle is part of a collection of magnets that Camille made for her grandfather.

Kraken; polymer; 4 x 6 inches (10 x 15cm). Camille transforms a familiar Earthbound enemy from a 2D video game character to a 3D sculpture.

El Goto mask; polymer; 6 inches tall (15cm). Bad temper and bad breath characterize this mask in the dragon series.

and working for herself was frustrating for the first few months. "Luckily my understanding and supportive husband encouraged me and helped build my confidence," she says, "and when I combined my love of video games and art I knew I'd found my perfect niche."

Camille's husband and his friends started up Fangamer.net, an online store dedicated to selling shirts and other merchandise inspired by video games. The group pooled their resources and talents to make a handbook for the game *Mother 3*, Camille's biggest project to date. Inspiration came from the original *EarthBound* player's guide, and they filled the handbook with photos of clay models, unusual game facts, and entertaining stories. No official art had been made for *Mother 3*, so Camille based the clay models on the tiny game sprites. It was a challenge that she thoroughly enjoyed. Camille uses polymer over wire-and-foil armatures to create original sculptures inspired by some of her other favorite video-game characters. She makes resin casts of the originals and hand-paints each one before offering it for sale online. Art permeates all areas of Camille's life, and she ventures beyond games, often using the plants and animals of Arizona as inspiration. Barbed wire and cactus are plentiful around her home, and as a child she spent a lot of time examining them up close. Camille's faux barbed wire was an online hit. "Recreating less dangerous versions in polymer has been fun," she says.

Even as her figurines have become more and more popular, she never forgets the inspiration and connection that her family has provided throughout her career in polymer. Camille explains, "Making art for my family and friends is more rewarding than shopping. For example, I continue to create magnets for my grandpa, who has a huge collection of my art on his fridge. These small gifts bring me some of the greatest joy."

Mustache; polymer; 9 inches tall (23cm). This mask shows Camille's ability to use a huge array of colors in a way that is simultaneously beautiful, complex, and detailed.

Cactus Bracelet; oil paint, Sculpey Superflex polymer, and liquid clay; 3 inch diameter (7.5cm).

Wind Fish Pin; Premo, liquid polymer, and oil paints; 2 inches wide (5cm).

Project:
Polymer Clay Illustration By Camille Young

In Camille's continuing quest to give the video-game world an added dimension through polymer, she shows us how she reinterprets characters from a game into wall art. This piece was inspired by the "Song of Storms," a recurring song of love and hope in *The Legend of Zelda* series of high-action fantasy video games. You can use this project as a guide for creating wall art of any characters who inspire you.

TOOLS AND MATERIALS

polymer clay in your choice of colors

paper and pencil for sketching

standard-size frame or shadow box (optional)

materials to create a background of your choice: collage papers, photographs, or paint

mat board or canvas board to fit the framecraft

X-Acto knife

large needle tool

tissue blade

polymer clay pattern cutters (Kemper)

clay-shaping tools (Colour Shapers)

wired ribbon (optional)

spray starch (optional)

hair dryer (optional)

clay gloss varnish

craft glue

INSTRUCTIONS

1 Make a sketch of the background as large as the final piece will be. Start thinking about the materials you'd like to use. Check ready-made frame sizes and choose to work in a standard size if you'd like to frame your final piece.

2 Sketch the clay pieces. I prefer to draw and cut these out so they're separate from the background. It's helpful to move the pieces around to find an arrangement you're happy with. These pieces could be characters, abstract designs, or anything else important to your scene. The planning stage isn't the most exciting part of the process, but it's necessary to prevent problems that might come up later. Allowing

enough time to plan will result in a more cohesive and polished final product.

3 Create the background, using collage, photograph, paint, or whatever else you'd like on your mat board or canvas. Just make sure the material is sturdy enough to support the clay pieces. For this piece I chose to paint on a small 6 × 8-inch (15 × 20.5cm) canvas.

4 Sculpt the clay pieces using your sketches as a guide. I like to use a craft blade, a large needle, a tissue blade, Kemper cutters, and an assortment of Colour Shaper tools. Cut out the basic geometric shapes for the character design from medium thin pieces of polymer

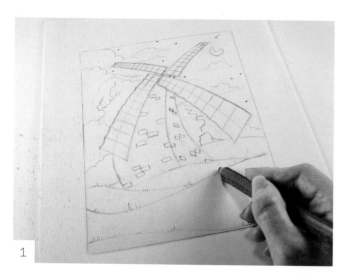

1

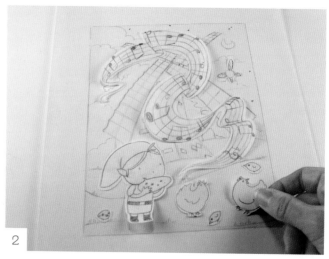

2

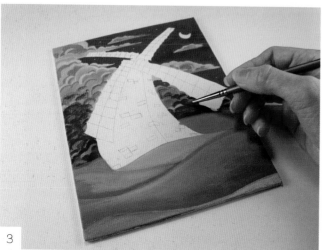

3

4

(3-4 playing cards) in the appropriate colors. Trim the pieces to the same size as your drawing. Butt the pieces together and gently smooth the seams. Add details with small rolls of clay (for the hair and arms), tiny balls (eyes), flat strips of color (belt, buckle, ears, hands, and boots). Draw on the clay with the needle tool to form details such as the nose and instrument's holes. Bake the clay according to the manufacturer's instructions.

5 Add any other nonclay element for a little texture and dimension. I used a wired ribbon and pinned it in the shape I wanted to a piece of cardboard. I applied two heavy coats of spray starch and dried it with a hair dryer. When removed from the cardboard, the ribbon retained its shape.

6 Add the final touches. I painted gloss varnish over the ocarina and the eyes to make them shiny.

7 Place the pieces where you want them and secure them with craft glue.

8 A shadow box or frame completes your picture.

5

6

7

8

RARELY
HAVE WE
SEEN A
PERSON
FAIL

life is a balance of holding on & letting go

CHAPTER 5

Small Scale

These artists show us how to shrink familiar objects into small tokens that are reminiscent of other times and places. Whether it's dollhouse-sized food, seen in Shay Aaron's popular jewelry, or small charms like Tejae Floyde's nested-heart tokens, small-scale art enjoys a big presence in the polymer world. Technical skill means a lot when it comes to finessing details at such a minute level, but the whimsy and emotional significance of these pieces are just as important.

Opposite, clockwise from top left:

Danielle Chandler, *Rarely Have We Seen*; polymer; 1 inch (2.5cm). Photograph by the artist. Danielle creates polymer sobriety tokens with a dark patina, customized for clients who wish to mark time or celebrate accomplishments.

Dawn Schiller, *Homunculus*; polymer, onyx beads, pocketwatch case, and powdered pigments; 2 inches (5cm). Photograph by the artist. A self-proclaimed lover of puns, Dawn specializes in fantasy characters, fugitives from fairy tales, and figments of her imagination.

Eva Thissen, *Little Red Riding Hood*; polymer clay brooch; 2 inches (5cm). Photograph by the artist. Eva, from Germany, recalls an entire story in a very small space using tiny bits of colorful polymer on a white ground.

Heather Wynn Millican, *Holding On and Letting Go*; polymer and copper ring finding; ¾ inch x 1¼ inches (2 x 3cm). Photograph by the artist. Enhanced with texture and patina, this ring bears a reminder for its owner.

Celine Roumagnac, *Village in the Clouds*; Deco brand polymer under glass; 5 inch (12.5cm) diameter under a 10 inch (25.5cm) dome. Photograph by the artist. Celine creates idyllic miniature scenes inspired by her French homeland and captures them in glass globes.

Cynthia Tinapple, *Granny Squares*; polymer; 2 inches (5 cm). Photograph by the artist. Rather than learn to crochet, Cynthia made faux crochet canes in polymer with a textured surface that mimics the look of yarn fibers.

Linda Cummings, *Salad Preparation*; polymer, wood, and glass; 1 inch diameter (2.5cm). Photograph by the artist.

Jen McGlon, *Valentine Luettes*; Super Sculpey polymer clay, acrylic paints, wire, vintage text, and glaze; 3 inches tall (7.5cm). Photograph by the artist. These nostalgic and stylized designs act as decorative, romantic reminders of simpler times and places.

Angie Scarr, *Melon Display*; polymer; 3 x 2 inches (7.5 x 5cm). Photograph by Frank Fisher. A recent transplant from the United Kingdom to Spain, Angie has started to look more closely at regional foods.

Erin Prais-Hintz, *One Day At a Time*; polymer charm in silverplate bezel; 1 inch tall (2.5cm). Photograph by the artist. The artist combines her love of words and jewelry in these modern day samplers featuring "simple truths."

Anita Behnen, *Flower Bug*; polymer and wire; 1 inch (2.5cm). Photograph by the artist. Anita packs her miniature bugs full of personality with endearing expressions.

Nikolina Otrzan, *My Pets*; polymer and markers; 1 x 2 inches (2.5 x 5cm). Photograph by the artist. The names of all of Nikolina's pets are written in stylized lettering on the surface of the pendant. The lettering makes an eye-catching design and a touching wearable memento by this artist from Zagreb, Croatia.

Pippa Chandler, *Beach Hut Bead*; polymer and acrylic paint; each ¾ x ½ inch (2cm x 13mm). These tiny cottages from the United Kingdom recall summer sun and days by the beach. The beads' textures are highlighted with acrylic paint and polished with Renaissance wax.

Linda Cummings, *Walnuts*; polymer and metal bowl; ¾ inch tall (2cm). Photograph by the artist. British artist Linda says her real food never looks as good as her mini reproductions.

Asvaneh Tajvidi, *Succulents*; polymer and wood; 1 inch (2.5cm). Photograph by the artist. Inspired by her windowsill garden, this Canadian artist, who goes by Afi, captures their blooms in miniature.

"Special foods have deep meanings for people." —SHAY AARON

Shay Aaron

Food for Thought ➤ Tel Aviv, Israel

From a very young age Shay Aaron had had a weight problem. "I was a really fat man who was depressed and miserable, but polymer helped me get over it," Shay recalls. He had been playing around with millefiori since he was nineteen, creating beads and home decor items, and eventually his two sisters showed him how to make simple jewelry that would appeal to women. When a customer asked him to create a replica of a traditional Jewish dish in miniature, he immediately knew he'd found what he wanted to do.

He transferred his addiction to unhealthy food into a passion for very small, very realistic miniature baked goods, tiny sumptuous meals for dollhouses, and wearable sweets. By the time he was twenty-three, his weight had climbed to 308 pounds; he credits polymer clay with saving his life. "It made me a happier, healthier person, and I lost 175 pounds," says Shay. Creating favorite traditional dishes in polymer also helped Shay relate to people all over the world. He discovered that food is endlessly inspirational and appeals to everyone. "Special foods have deep meanings for people, and I can create small, noncaloric reminders of festive family times," he added.

Shay's best ideas come on Friday mornings when he works with his mother in her little kitchen in Tel Aviv. "Every Friday evening we host the whole family, and my mom is in charge of the cooking. My assignment is to come up with a special dessert that complements her dishes, and these ideas often inspire designs for jewelry," he says. He doesn't often visit restaurants but instead browses the Internet, where the ideas are endless. Narrowing his focus to special and traditional cuisines makes his research easier. Shay starts with sketches from photos he's collected for inspiration, a collection of creative dishes he sees online and thumbing through magazines and books. Because he works in precise 1:12 dollhouse scale, measurements and details like color and texture have to be accurate to produce realistic miniature food.

"My customers have to have a sense of humor and be open-minded. Not everyone is comfortable wearing salmon-steak earrings or a veggie necklace," he laughs. That his pieces are reasonably priced and fun to wear brings him even more pleasure.

Several years ago Shay wanted to connect with other artists so he searched online for "polymer clay" in Hebrew and found the Israeli Polymer Clay Guild. "Now some of my best friends are polymer clay artists. I never knew there were so many people who shared my interests." Once a year the guild members meet to attend a conference. Through one of these conferences, Shay taught a three-day workshop in Normandy, France, where he met people who follow his work, and received invitations to teach in other countries.

Opposite, clockwise from top left:

Shay Aaron in his Tel Aviv studio.

Seder Plate; polymer; 1 inch across (2.5cm). Shay's replica of the ritual centerpiece of Passover.

Fresh Vegetable Platter; polymer vegetables with wood base. Cabbage is 11/16 inch (1.7cm). Shay shares his red cabbage cane instructions online.

Beet Earrings; polymer with silver findings; 6/8 inch long (1.9cm).

With obvious pride, Shay shakes his head and says, "Sometimes my life is like a dream, and I can't believe it's possible. I started playing with polymer in 2001. Last year I was teaching abroad, and people all over the world were purchasing my work."

Today Shay teaches polymer and miniature making for a living, but he has pursued other interests as well. He completed a degree in pastry studies with the intention of becoming a pastry chef, thinking he wanted to create edible desserts in addition to jewelry. But after a few months, he knew that pastry making was not his passion, and he began studying set and costume design for stage and film. Shay says, "No matter what I do after I finish my studies, I will continue to create mini treats and will somehow combine polymer clay in my future work."

Seder Table; wood furniture, ceramic, and polymer. In addition to being worn as jewelry, Shay's miniatures perfectly suit 1:12 dollhouses and miniature scenes.

Making Pizza; polymer, wood, and glass bottle; pizza is 2¼ inch diameter (5.7 cm). The dime in the middle of the scene illustrates the scale of the small tableau. Polymer canes reduce perfectly to tiny diameters and allow Shay to create very realistic food.

Project:
Pizza Charm By Shay Aaron

What food says "fun" better than pizza? Shay Aaron introduces you to the small pleasures of miniatures with his easy-to-follow pizza recipe. If you don't want to wear your treat, there's certainly a dollhouse that would love a pizza delivery. Remember, you're working small, so the specific quantities of clay are not noted here. The pictures are the best indicator of the amount you will need.

TOOLS AND MATERIALS

polymer clay: small amounts in terra-cotta, brown, red, translucent, white, yellow, and ocher, plus other colors as desired for toppings (such as green for peppers)

single-edge razor blade

rough sandpaper

paintbrush

chalk pastels in ocher and brown

scrap of card stock

liquid polymer clay

small container

red acrylic paint

toothpick

jewelry findings (optional)

INSTRUCTIONS

 To make the pepperoni cane, combine shades of terra-cotta, brown, and red polymer clay with a mix of three-fourths translucent and one-fourth white. Roughly chop all polymer clay parts into each other.

 Combine the clay colors into one single cane and chop again if necessary to achieve the marbled effect of pepperoni. Reduce the pepperoni cane to about ¼ inch (6mm) in diameter. Bake the mini pepperoni cane according to the manufacturer's instructions for 10 minutes.

 For the pizza dough, mix white polymer clay with a pinch of yellow and ocher. Form a ¾-inch (2cm) ball. Flatten the ball against rough sandpaper; this gives a nice texture to the bottom of your pizza. Continue shaping the crust by pulling up and smoothing the edges. Now use the sandpaper to texture the crust of your pizza.

 Rub the ocher and brown-colored chalk pastels on a scrap of card stock and use a dry brush to pick up the pigment and apply it to the "dough" to create a nicely toasted crust color. Cut out a triangular slice and bake the entire crust for 10 minutes.

1

2

3

4

5 While the pizza dough is baking, mix together 1 part white with a small amount of ocher polymer clay for a cheese color. Condition the clay until it's warm and soft. Pour a few drops of liquid polymer clay in a small container and blend it with the cheese-colored clay. Stir the clays together until everything is blended and you get a nice icing-textured mixture.

6 Paint the center of your pizza with small amount of red acrylic paint to create the sauce. Let it dry.

7 Add the melting cheese on top of the dried "pizza sauce" you created with acrylic paint. Spread it around on your pizza using a toothpick. Add slices from the baked pepperoni cane (see step 2) and any other toppings that suit your crowd. I've added some curved green polymer shavings to simulate peppers. Bake for 10 minutes.

8 Once the pizza has cooled, mix a small amount of liquid polymer clay with a very small bit of ocher and brown chalk-pastel powders. Brush your pizza with the colored liquid clay to get a toasted effect. Add jewelry findings, if desired, and bake for 30 minutes. Enjoy!

5

6

7

8

"Making things with our hands is as natural as breathing." —TEJAE FLOYDE

Tejae Floyde
Pocket Art ▸ Colorado, United States

Tejae Floyde knows the healing power of small-scale objects, and nothing brings her more pleasure than creating those kinds of mementos for others. The first jewelry Tejae Floyde ever received was a heart-shaped birthstone ring from her father when she was four years old. She remembers the small ring fondly and held onto it as charm for luck and protection throughout a very difficult childhood. As a polymer artist, she has become known for her small hearts, often hearts contained within hearts that are decorated with swirling gold designs. She sometimes hides messages inside.

Tejae comes from a family of makers and artists. She never had any trouble calling herself an artist. "I'm part Cherokee Indian and Irish from my father's side, and making things with our hands is as natural as breathing," she explains. She and her brother made a game out of collecting miniature trinkets when they were kids, and they created toys out of everything. "I remember my dad teaching us to make a paintbrush from a twig of a mimosa tree. We'd mix a little water with the common red clay rocks. We would spend countless hours 'painting' our little metal Tonka trucks with this mixture. These early experiences helped form my creativity. I have a collection of small boxes that remind me of my brother, and I still enjoy making art out of a lump of clay," she says.

Tejae's path to polymer has a winding one, with various artistic dreams, personal setbacks, and triumphs. At thirteen, she saw a greeting-card catalog featuring illustrated artwork and fantasized that she would someday be an artist working there. After a difficult adolescence in which she left home, and a marriage that ended badly, Tejae reunited with her mother. At nineteen, she began working for the catalog company she had dreamed about, and twenty-four years later she's still there, now as product manager for the company. She remarried in 2004 and says that she leads a charmed life. After seeing a heart-shaped purse by Kathleen Dustin in a Colorado gallery in 2000, Tejae was inspired to try polymer. She started reading books on polymer and joined Pikes Peak Polymer Clay guild, where Donna Kato was a member. "I've learned techniques from some of the most talented guild members, but I dislike making something someone else has already made. Even in workshops I have to change the project and make it my own," she says.

While her small hearts may inspire her to create larger projects, the idea of secrets and surprises will always be central to her story. As a child, Tejae kept many things to herself, and like most kids, she felt she caused the problems around her. She acknowledges that "secrets used to be about hiding, but now they're about sharing—sharing what's in your heart even when you're afraid to say it because you might get rejected. It's important to me to be able to help people say those things." Objects that have layers and aren't exactly what they appear to be intrigue her. She thinks about "the mechanics of the Russian nested dolls. Like unwrapping a gift, the anticipation of finding what's inside makes you smile."

Opposite, clockwise from top left:

Tejae Floyde in her Colorado Springs home studio. Photograph by Chris Gosnell.

Mary's Heart; polymer, image transfer, and rhinestone; 1½ inches (3.8cm). Tejae further embellishes her hearts and rebakes them after the initial forms are created and baked.

Enchanting Crown Boxes; polymer with metallic finish; 2 x 3 inches (5 x 7.5cm). Tejae creates containers that can hold treasures or secrets.

Free Spirit; polymer; 1½ inches (3.8cm). Tejae subscribes to the belief, "It's the little things that count."

Tejae's most-requested items are memorial hearts made as tributes to people who have passed. She loves the fact that "these hearts bring back a fond memory of a loved one and give you something to touch that reminds you that the person was here." When Tejae is experimenting with a design, instead of wearing it for the whole world to see, she'll slip it into her coat pocket. Sometimes her husband, Tim, will notice her sly smile and ask, "Do you have something in your pocket?" She admits, "It brings me joy to know it's there, feel it, take it out and look at it. I hope I'll graduate from that feeling to being able to wear my work." Tejae works full-time and looks forward to having more time to spend on polymer. She is building a portfolio, working with a coach to help her focus and shape the future of her art, teaching online, and expanding her classes.

Hearing her customers' stories, memories, and celebrations keeps Tejae going. "Being a part of their stories energizes me. I get to celebrate fun times and bring some comfort to people. That is a pretty cool deal."

Wedding Hearts; polymer with wire; each 1½ inches (3.8cm). These inscribed hearts make memorable ornaments.

Romantic Heart; polymer; 1½ inches (3.8cm). The closure on this piece follows the curve of the medallion.

Project:
Simple Encased Heart By Tejae Floyde

You can find important messages and powerful emotions in the smallest of tokens. Tejae Floyde shows you the basic method she developed to create her popular encased hearts, containing mysteries that reveal themselves as they're opened. This project begs for you to put your own spin on it. You can embellish these simple hearts with any surface designs you'd like. And if two hearts aren't enough, add more layers.

TOOLS AND MATERIALS

polymer clay (I prefer Premo) in at
    least 2 colors of your choice

glass work surface

bone folder or similar clay-shaping
    tool

flame-retardant polyester batting

baking tile

aluminum foil

scissors

pasta machine

texture sheets or stamp (optional)

spray bottle with water (optional)

acrylic rod (optional)

tissue blade

marker

INSTRUCTIONS

1. Shape half a block of conditioned clay into a ball. Roll the bottom of the ball more aggressively between your palms to create a teardrop shape. Use your fingers to assist you in forming the teardrop if necessary.

2. Crease the top of the teardrop in the middle and shape the heart's two humps using a bone folder or a clay-shaping tool. At this point you can stamp the inside heart with decorative symbols or words if desired.

3. Place the heart onto a piece of flame-retardant polyester batting and a baking tile. Bake according to the manufacturer's instructions for approximately 20 minutes. Allow the piece to cool.

4. Place the baked heart on a piece of aluminum foil folded in half. Cut around the heart, leaving ¼ inch (6mm) of foil beyond the heart. Start with the under-side and smooth the foil flat against the heart. Use your bone folder or clay-shaping tool to press the foil into the heart's crease.

1

2

3

4

5 Continue smoothing the foil on the top side of the heart. The covered heart should look similar to the photo.

6 Roll half a block of conditioned clay through your pasta machine at the thick setting (7–8 playing cards). If you want to embellish this layer, lightly spray a texture sheet with water and place the sheet of clay against the texture sheet. Press clay into the texture sheet using an acrylic rod. (An alternative is to roll a texture sheet with the clay through the pasta machine.) Wrap the foil-covered heart. I find it easiest to wrap the heart by positioning half the clay layer on each side.

7 Use scissors to cut away any excess clay.

8 Pinch the sides together. Smooth the seams lightly with your fingers.

5

6

7

8

9 You can hide imperfections and seams by smoothing the heart, pressing it against a glass work surface. Take a break and set your heart aside for 10-15 minutes to allow it to cool and stiffen up a bit. This will make the clay easier to slice with the flexible blade.

10 Pick up the heart with your nondominant hand. Hold it carefully, with your fingers supporting the top and bottom. Pick up your tissue blade with your dominant hand.

11 Start with the blade on the left side of the heart. Pivot the blade to the far right side while you pivot the heart to the left. Using medium pressure, slice the outer shell evenly all the way around the heart. The trick is to keep your blade straight so you only make one cut. Leave the blade in the heart and turn your heart around. Aim before you cut again: Look for the cut edge that you need to meet up with and target your blade to meet that previously cut line. Don't press too hard or you'll cut the baked heart inside. Lightly smooth out any fingerprints.

12 Place the covered heart onto the polyester batting and a tile. Bake according to the manufacturer's instructions for approximately 20 minutes.

9

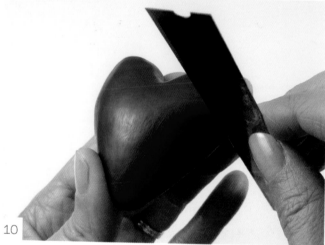

10

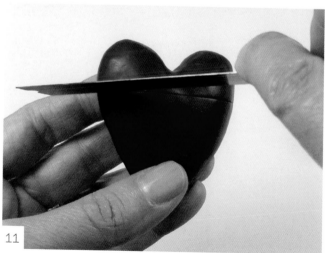

11

12

13 Remove the nested hearts from the oven and allow the piece to cool for 10 minutes. While the piece is still slightly warm, lightly twist the top along the cut line. Gently wiggle and prod it. If it won't budge, use your blade to lightly cut through the top layer of clay. Use light pressure or you will cut through to the inner heart.

14 Pull out the encased heart and remove the aluminum foil.

15 Because this is a handmade piece, the case will only go together one way. Mark the lip of the top and bottom pieces with a dot to make it easy to line up the dots and put the case back together again.

13

14

15

CHAPTER 6

Large Scale

This chapter concentrates on polymer art in a larger format, created by artists with strong and boldly executed visions. Because their installations are more often shown in galleries and museums, artists working at this scale help to elevate craft to the level of art. They are able to reach out to a broader audience who may be exposed to polymer for the first time. Gera Scott Chandler, working with polymer on canvas, demonstrates how to build an infrastructure that can accommodate large-scale pieces. For these artists who see polymer in the wider context of the art world, bigger is better. It's time to dream big.

Opposite, clockwise from top left:

Laura Tabakman, *Polymer Vessel*; polymer clay and steel wire; 20 x 9 x 4 inches (50 x 23 x 10cm). President of the Pittsburgh Polymer Clay Guild, Laura often integrates fiber, photography, and polymer into three-dimensional pieces and installations for galleries and juried shows.

Meredith Dittmar, *Theophanic Imagination*; polymer and acrylic; 23 x 18 inches (58 x 45.5cm). Created for this American artist's solo show, titled *Now You See It*, in Mexico City, this piece is enclosed in its own custom-made shadow box.

Angelika Arendt, *Untitled*; polymer; 9 x 7 x 6 inches (23 x 18 x 15cm). Working in Berlin, and Karlsruhe, Germany, Angelika creates fantastical sculptures that resemble coral reefs, which can fill entire gallery spaces.

Wendy Wallin Malinow, *Sugar Skull Teapot*, 2012; polymer clay. Photograph by Courtney Frisse. A Portland native, Wendy created this "dysfunctional teapot" for an exhibit of teapots at the Mobilia Gallery in Cambridge, Massachusetts.

Joan Israel, *Formal Garden*; polymer on canvas; 12 x 16 inches (30.5 x 41cm). A member of the New York Polymer Guild, Joan's mind-boggling compositions of intricate polymer canes evoke the tropical atmosphere of the French painter Henri Rousseau.

Heather Campbell, *He Said, She Said*; polymer, acrylic, beads, and found objects; 19 x 23 x 8 inches (48 x 58 x 20cm). Bright colors and rich detail surround two clowns who may have had a slight difference of opinion in this playful piece.

Alev Gozonar, *Marilyn VIP*; polymer; 35 x 50 inches (89 x 127cm). In the gallery, polymer QR codes were placed next to each portrait to encourage audience interaction in this piece from Istanbul, Turkey.

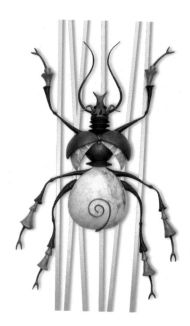

Francoise Guitton, *Insecte 20*; polymer; 20 x 20 inches (50 x 50cm). While this French artist is also known for her fashion-inspired illustrations (see page 25), this intricate, oversized beetle showcases her immense technical skill.

◄ Peggy Dembicer, *ARTnews*, 2012; polymer, seed and bugle beads, semiprecious bits, studs, and paint; 13 x 15 inches (33 x 38cm). Conneticut-based artist Peggy is inspired by cultural artifacts such as magazine covers as well as beadwork by the Huichol Indians of Mexico.

➤ Rachel Gourley, *Doodle 3*; polymer in driftwood; 2 inches (5cm) each. Rachel's installations are inspired by the Vancouver coast. A former scientific illustrator from Yorkshire, England, she is a world traveler who has lived in Abu Dhabi, the Balkans, and Brussels.

Joan Israel, *Tequila Bottle*; polymer and glass; 8 inches (20cm). Joan upcycles base materials into art, using a glass bottle as an armature on which to build this imaginative landscape.

Rachel Gourley, *Sand Dollars*; polymer; each 2 inches in diameter (5cm). Rachel was drawn to polymer in part because it travels well and allowed her to be creative during periods when she and her family were frequently traveling the globe.

Adam Thomas Rees, *Winter's Bear*; polymer and wire base; 5 x 3 x 2 feet. Assembled with a variety of canes, this piece was created for the Face of Utah Sculpture VII, in 2011. Adam credits his growing up in the American West as a major influence on his work.

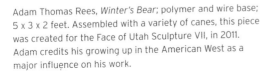

"If I need an idea about a subject I look at how kids see it first." —GERA SCOTT CHANDLER

Gera Scott Chandler

Shorelines ▸ British Columbia, Canada

Gera Chandler has lived on a rocky beach since she was a toddler, and growing up she was either walking through the bush or on the beach, drawing. The beach is still at the center of her art. Her jewelry, sculpture, and wall art frequently feature water, fish, and her "beach muse."

Gera's work is recognized for her luminous "scritch-scratch" sheets that she sometimes covers with layers of resin for a dichroic glass look. To avoid repetitive work, she has developed methods of using sheets of collaged veneers that can be cut up and applied to a variety of necklaces and bracelets. Jewelry provides the stable base of her business, but she prefers making larger, more ambitious polymer vessels, lamps, wall sculptures, baskets, and three-dimensional pieces. Even when she is building inventory for shows and galleries, she infuses every piece with a sense of spontaneity.

Bright color, biomorphic forms, and organic shapes all appear in Gera's work, reflecting her years teaching art in elementary school and her love for the work of Austrian artist Friedensreich Hundertwasser. "If I'm really stuck for an approach, I'll search online for kids' art. Children get the most important lines down quickly. If I need an idea about a subject I look at how kids see it first."

Gera's daughter has Asperger's syndrome, which kept Gera close to home, where she experimented with graphic design, paper and gourd arts, stamp carving, and soap making before discovering polymer. She was looking for a way to drill holes in beach stones in an early online community when Texas artist Marty Woosley urged her to explore the imitative capabilities of polymer clay. Polymer met every requirement on Gera's wish list for a perfect medium: It offered color, sculpture, immediacy, and portability, and it could be done at home with two small children. She soon hooked up with the Clayamies, or Canadian Polymer Clay Friends, whose two names reflect Canada's bilingual culture.

These days, Gera gets up early and heads to her studio in the upstairs of their house, built in 1911, just a five-minute walk from the beach in Victoria. She speaks every day with a gallery owner-artist friend in Westport, Ontario, and with other polymer friends, including artist Wanda Shum, who lives nearby and creates her designs with polymer millefiori.

Gera calls herself the world's worst Etsy seller, preferring direct contact with gallery owners and show customers over online promotion. "I get discouraged by thin online sales and don't want to invest the time required to make it work," she says. There's more buzz about polymer and a larger market not far away, but complications make it difficult for Canadian artists like Gera to teach in the United States.

Meanwhile, Gera is exploring methods to integrate polymer into her basket making, sometimes using kelp harvested from the nearby ocean and other beach finds. While basket making allows her to craft objects on a larger scale, she can't imagine leaving polymer behind. "There's always something new and interesting, and polymer is too much a part of my social network to ever think about leaving."

Opposite, clockwise from top left:

Gera Chandler in her upstairs home studio in Victoria.

The Flower Seller; polymer; 11 x 14 inches (28 x 35.5cm). Gera is known for striking, luminous color in her polymer pieces.

Ring; polymer, foils, inks, and resin in silver bezel.

Suspended Vessel 2; polymer, alcohol inks, and copper wire; 14 x 5 inches (35.5 x 12.5cm). Gera combines polymer and basket making.

Project:
Inked Polymer-Clay Still Life

By Gera Scott Chandler

Borrowing techniques from both painting and polymer, Gera creates a hybrid work of art. In the following project, she divulges the secret to her "scritch-scratch" look, using a combination of texturing, carving, and painting to achieve a gorgeously layered surface that seems to glow with color. With a bigger canvas as a base, this approach to polymer can be adjusted to create large-scale works. The only limit is your imagination (and the size of your oven!)

TOOLS AND MATERIALS

polymer clay in translucent and black, 4 ounces (113.5g) of each, plus scrap clay for positioning still-life elements

paper and pencil for sketching

stretched canvas or wooden cradleboard, 1 × 4 × 4 inches (2.5 × 10 × 10cm)

scissors

pasta machine

plastic wrap

metallic leaf sheets (gold, silver, copper, or a combination)

spoon or other burnishing tool

X-Acto knife

needles, stamps, or any items for making interesting scratches and impressions on the clay surface

alcohol inks

paintbrushes

needle tool

micro Phillips screwdriver (optional)

small, round cutter (optional)

liquid decorating gel (Fimo)

needle or straight pin (optional)

wire (optional)

NOTE

The thickness of the translucent level is optional. A very thin layer will reveal more foil, while a thicker sheet will make the foiling subtler and your colors more intense.

INSTRUCTIONS

1. Make your sketch to fit the exact size of your canvas. I like to place the canvas directly on the paper and trace around it. Use the side of the canvas to draw a margin that makes an allowance for the sides of the canvas.

2. Create 2 sketches, or master sheets, that will help you to determine the scale as you draw your components on the clay. The first sketch helps as you draw the fruits and the bowl freehand onto your clay. The second sketch shows the background and foreground pieces, including the margins. Cut this second sketch into 2 separate pieces.

3. Run 4 ounces (113.5g) of translucent clay through the pasta machine at a thickness of 6 playing cards. Place the clay on a sheet of plastic wrap and cover it with foil leaf. Run 4 ounces (113.5g) of black clay at a 4 playing-card thickness. Cover the foil with the black clay, then cover the whole stack with plastic wrap and burnish with a spoon. Flip over the plastic wrap and the stack and repeat the burnishing process.

4. Use your paper templates as a guide to cut the background and foreground sections. Place your templates carefully to conserve the stacked clay. With the X-Acto knife, cut 4 squares from the corners to accommodate the corners of the canvas. Texture the foreground with a pointed texture tool of your choice using a horizontal stroke to give a grounded effect. Texture the background using vertical strokes that suggest a wall or draping. Ink the foreground in green and teal tones with a horizontal motion, and the background in purple tones with a vertical flow.

1

2

3

4

5 Using the shape template, trace the vessel and fruit onto the clay with a needle tool. Freehand extra pieces of fruit with your paintbrush and inks, inventing as you go. I added peaches and plums at this point. Use stamps, needles, and texture sheets to scritch-scratch the surface of the clay. The more detail the better! Use a needle to poke tiny holes all over the oranges for a wonderful realistic-skin effect, and use a micro Phillips screwdriver to stamp tiny stems. Ink the vessel and fruit components and let them dry before cutting them out.

6 A simple way to deal with all those grapes is to use a small round cutter to define each grape on the sheet. Add inks with a fine brush. When the ink is dry, cover with plastic wrap and use the cutter again to punch out each grape. Each grape will be nicely rounded, and you can do a bit of manipulation to adjust the size and shape for each one to add variety.

7 Cut out the components. Slant your cutting blade at a sharp beveled angle and cut out each piece of fruit and the vessel. Press down the beveled edges of the clay, which will give your clay a nice rounded effect.

8 Prepare the canvas by spreading a layer of Fimo gel over it.

9 Slide the background and foreground sections in place, being sure that there are no gaps between them. Join the corners and press into position. Press

5

6

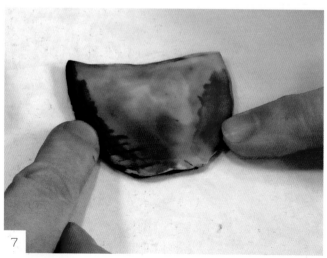

7

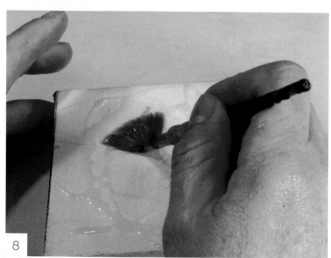

8

or use a pin to remove air bubbles and fire the canvas for 10 minutes to set the clay.

10 Use your tracing to as a guide for placing the items on the canvas. Coat the base of the container shape with Fimo gel and place the base flat on the canvas. Shape black or scrap clay to place under the container to raise it from the canvas surface. Use more Fimo gel as required. Be sure that the sides of the vessel rest on the canvas; the rim or lip of the container will have a gap so the fruit can "sit" in the container.

11 The fruit will be added to the composition in two layers. The first layer goes directly on the canvas. There will be gaps. Do not overlap.

12 Each item in the next layer will have a small ball of clay behind it to raise it from the surface and give a three-dimensional effect. Use this layer to cover the gaps on the lower level that sits against the canvas.

13 The pieces of fruit at the top of the pile extend past the canvas. This section should be reinforced with a section of black clay behind the pieces. The stem and leaf that are a quirky point of interest can be reinforced with a careful insertion of wire. To maximize translucence, you may want to fire the entire piece one last time for just a few minutes. Take the heated polymer-covered canvas out of the oven and plunge it in cold water. A quick cold bath makes the clay clearer and the colors more vibrant.

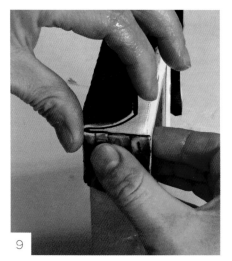

9

10

11

12

13

CHAPTER 7

Beadworks

Contemporary polymer beadwork hearkens back to ancient times, when beads were used as talisman, currency, and personal adornment. In today's world, it can also act as social currency to benefit a community, teach skills, and promote artistic independence. "Look good, feel good, and do good" is the motto of the Samunnat Project, founded by Wendy Moore and local Nepalis, and this exposure to another culture has changed Wendy's personal art. Meanwhile, Rebecca Watkins crafts individual precious beads that travel the world to be combined by other artists into unique jewelry. The cross-cultural art in this section demonstrates how polymer beads can build community and improve lives.

Opposite, clockwise from top left:

Corliss Rose and John Lemieux Rose, *Absolem's Fete Necklace*; polymer; 22 inches (56cm). This duo thought they would make a few simple beads and they fell down the bead-making rabbit hole, creating an entire series inspired by *Alice in Wonderland*.

Margit Böhmer, *Denim Coral Necklace*; polymer, blue sponge coral, glass beads, and silver clasp; 20 inches (50cm). Inspired by beadwork from Tibet and Africa, Margit is a self-taught artist in Germany who has learned from visiting American masters.

Marcia Tzigelnik, *Polka Dot Flower Beads*, 2012; polymer with metal trimmed centers. Working from Israel, Marcia is able to reach an international market by keeping an active shop on the website Etsy, where she sells both finished jewelry and premade canes.

Cynthia Tinapple and Erin Prais-Hintz, *Tibetan Dreams Necklace*. Erin added turquoise, coral, amber, and silver beads to Cynthia's polymer pumpkin-shaped beads to create an asymmetric necklace as a prototype for the Samunnat Project (page 125).

Cynthia Tinapple, *Shisha Shields Necklace*; polymer and mirrors; 25 inches (63.5cm). The textured surface resembles a crazy quilt.

Scott Mizevitz, *Bottle of Hope*; polymer and glass; 4 inches (10cm). Started by a Rhode Island-based survivor of cancer, the Bottles of Hope and Beads of Courage projects give these works of art to cancer patients. They symbolize hope for a healthy future.

Ron Lehocky, *Check Your Heart*, 2012; polymer; 2 x 3 inches (5 x 7.5cm). A beloved pediatrician, Ron's heart brooches caught on in his Louisville, Kentucky, community, where galleries and shops sell them to support the local Kids' Center.

Cheryl L. Ploegstra, *Stroppel Scrap Beads*;
polymer; ½ to ¾ inch (13mm to 2cm).
Photograph by the artist. Cheryl puts a spin
on the ubiquitous rolled paper bead by using
scrap polymer and a method developed by
Alice Stroppel (see page 9).

Vera Kleist, *Purple Rough Cut Extruder Beads Necklace*; polymer with silver clasp; 20 inches (50cm). Photograph by the artist. Germany artist Vera carved into polymer to create this look. Like Rebecca Watkins (page 135), she also sells individual beads to jewelry makers.

Ron Lehocky, *For the Kids Center*; polymer;
1 x 2 inches (2.5 x 5cm) each. Photograph
by the artist. Making thousands of hearts
for charity, Ron has tried every technique in
existence and accepts scrap clay from other
artists to incorporate into his own designs.

"We all need to create."

—WENDY MOORE

Wendy Moore

Flourishing ▸ Broken Hill, Australia, and Birtamod, Nepal

When she was growing up, Wendy trekked through Nepal with her family on a vacation that would have far-reaching effects on her career as an artist. Only fifteen years old, she fell in love with the Sherpas' culture and decided that she would marry one. Although she grew her hair long and wore it in two long braids to look Tibetan, a Sherpa husband wasn't in the cards. She became a speech pathologist, married Malcolm (a doctor), and settled down in Albury, Australia. At home in the evenings, she retreated to her polymer studio. "I felt greedy and guilty not doing things with my friends in order to get into my special room," she says, "but I'd get irritable if I couldn't spend time with clay."

Wendy worked with mothers of children with brain injuries, and sometimes she taught these women how to create polymer jewelry. On counseling and workshop follow-up forms, they often reported that the clay lesson was their favorite and the most helpful activity—sometimes this was the first time in years that they'd done something for themselves. "We just don't play anymore," they admitted. "For the first time in a long time I'm doing something more than being the mother of a brain-injured boy," one mother said. Wendy realized the power of creativity and making. "I'm almost evangelical now about it," says Wendy. "We all need to create."

Over the years Wendy's hearing had become impaired, and a bout of a serious illness in 2007 sharpened her appreciation of the swiftness of life. She and her husband decided to return to Nepal, where he would teach in a medical school and Wendy would find something to entertain herself. She brought along her polymer clay so that she could at least have something to work on all day. Some friends introduced her to the Samunnat Project, a small nonprofit, nonreligious, nonpolitical organization for abused women in the eastern region of Nepal. Samunnat, a word that means "flourishing" in Nepali, was formed by a group of friends who had each been approached for help by women trying to escape domestic violence or trafficking. The future cofounders realized that they could help more by forming a group than they could by assisting individually.

The project set up training programs to build confidence and give the women skills. Wendy resisted the idea of teaching the women polymer. "The clay's not readily available, it's not sustainable, it's very Western, and it won't be workable in this warm climate," she argued. But she soon learned that the market was flooded with seed-bead items, and polymer clay jewelry stood out. One day, a fair-trade vendor pointed to the polymer pendant on Wendy's neck and said, "I could sell that." So Wendy started to enlist travelers and vendors who would bring polymer to Nepal and began to teach. "Even if the ladies are just having some happy times, that's okay," she remembers. "If I had waited for the perfectly sustainable, endlessly successful project, I never would have done anything. I decided to give it a year to see what would happen."

Opposite, clockwise from top left:

Wendy Moore at home in her studio in Broken Hill, New South Wales, Australia.

After the Monsoon Necklace; polymer and glass beads. This necklace celebrates the lush vegetation that blooms in Nepal after the rains.

Ruby Lariat Pendant; polymer, Nepali wedding beads, and silver finding; 30 inches (76.2cm).

Thakali Women; polymer and seed beads; 4 inches (10cm). Wendy was inspired by the Thakali women of the Annapurna region.

The ladies loved creating with polymer. They covered all their costs and received a fare wage, while Wendy could see a sense of pride blossom in all of them. "We feel like we're artists and not victims," they would say. "You could see their self-pride blossom," Wendy added. Locals started visiting their studio (which, at first, was basically a garage facing the highway) and marveled at the intricate beads that these women, some of them untouchables, were creating.

On a practical level, the women found that if they told their families, "I'm leaving my husband because he's beating me, and I'm earning an income on my own," their confidence made it more likely that the family would be supportive, knowing that the artist could contribute financially. Families who were initially hostile to the project began telling other women in the village who were being abused that they didn't have to put up with that treatment, referring them to Samunnat. Wendy noticed a ripple effect throughout the community.

After four years living in Nepal, Wendy and her husband returned to Australia, but with a plan to return Nepal twice every year, when she could lead visitors on tours and assist

Samunnat. "I had been passionate about my brain injury work, but I didn't want to be relied on so heavily again. With Samunnat, I was able to be part of a team without having to run the whole show. It's really good that I'm not there all the time. They've got to work things out, and in the months when I'm gone, there's so much going on."

The women are selling their wares online through Etsy and in galleries in Australia. They train new artists entering the project and have even set up their own micro-lending system. Polymer artists have visited to teach them advanced skills, and people around the world have contributed time, money, and support to the project.

Wendy's own polymer art has grown as well, reflecting her strong identification with the culture. Wendy had always loved the look of Tibetan jewelry with its little compartments, amulets, and religious significance. "I love the scale of the jewelry and the fact that it isn't just for ornamentation. Women in Nepal might wear amber beads the size of eggs. It has significance and is worn with abandon." Wendy continues to share her love of traditional crafts and traveling, as her childhood love has given her the opportunity to flourish.

Terai Sunset Necklace; Kato polymer, Nepali wedding beads, and silver clasp; 20 inches (50cm).

Black and White Disc Necklace; Kato polymer and Nepali wedding beads; 21 inches (53cm).

Red, Black, and White Sampler Necklace; Kato polymer, Nepali wedding beads, and silver clasp; 20 inches (50cm).

Project:
Tibetan Tube Necklace By Wendy Moore

This project celebrates a rich, colorful, ancient, and—tragically—threatened culture. The colors and motifs in Buddhist temple decorations inspired this project, and the multiple strands of seed beads are a very traditional Nepali style. These instructions give you information for the basic components and then suggest variations. Wendy hopes this encourages you to come up with your own particular response to this amazing culture. Change the shape of the tubes, swap colors, and alter bead shapes.

TOOLS AND MATERIALS

polymer clay (Kato) in colors mixed according
   to the color chart on page 128

plus well-mixed scrap clay

plastic bags and labels for storage

ruler or measuring tape

dowel, ¾ inch (2cm) in diameter

parchment paper

pasta machine

liquid polymer clay

X-Acto knife

texturing blocks (I use a piece of a ceramic
   foot pumice and a Tibetan wood block)

sandpaper

acrylic paint in gold

soft cloth

gold leaf

Pearl Ex gold (optional)

tissue blade

needle

seed bead strands, chain or necklace cording
   of your choice (optional)

TIP

I use Kato clay because it is really
durable after baking and copes better
with the monsoon humidity in Nepal.
You may need to jiggle the color
recipes a bit if you use other clays.

INSTRUCTIONS

 Condition and mix your colors following the color chart below. Prepare 4 ounces (113.5g) of the white mix and 2 ounces (56g) of the others. Keep any leftovers in labeled plastic bags. Roll your white mix into a long tube approximately ⅛ inch (3mm) wide and 4½ inches (11.5cm) long. If it is warm, pop it in the fridge to make it easier to slice.

 Use black clay or well-mixed dark scrap clay to create the inner core of all your components. I make these on a dowel ¾ inch (2cm) in diameter that has been wrapped with a twist of baking or parchment paper to make it easy to remove the clay after baking.

Roll your clay to a medium-thick setting (5-6 playing cards) and cut 1 strip that is 1 3/16 inches (3cm) wide and 4 strips that are ⅜ inch (10mm) wide. I usually make as many as I can and save them for when I need them. I use cardboard templates and a homemade grid chart to keep the sizes consistent and lines straight. Wrap the strips lightly around the dowel and seal the join where the two ends meet by pinching and smoothing it with your fingers. These rings will be the cores for the beads.

Bake the cores and allow them to cool in the oven. When they are completely cool, slide them off the dowel. If they resist, slide the paper twist off the dowel to remove. Sand the edges lightly.

1

2

COLOR CHART	
White Mix	equal parts white, pearl, and translucent
Red Chili	12 parts red, 2 parts magenta, 1 part silver, 1 part pearl
Persimmon	equal parts orange and red
Sea Green	3 parts green, 1 part blue
Pink Chili	6 parts red, 6 parts magenta, 1 part silver, 1 part pearl
Ultra Blue	Kato blue

TIP

At Samunnat, we use color labeling devised by polymer artist team Dave and Carolyn Good. This system helps when we're discussing colors long-distance. Some of the colors used here are the Goods' recipes. Thanks, guys.

3 To create the red and gold bead, first spread a very thin layer of liquid clay polymer on 2 of the ³⁄₈-inch (10mm) cores. Roll out some of your red chili clay on the pasta machine's medium-thin setting (1–2 playing cards) and cut a strip slightly wider than the prebaked core. Cover the core with the red strip, pressing lightly to remove air bubbles. Carefully seal the join where the two clay ends meet using your fingers, but to ensure its strength, make sure you don't put the red chili join directly over the join of the core. Press the edges gently so they adhere and cover the black edges of the core.

4 Use an X-Acto knife to trim the excess so that you can't see the black of the tube.

5 With the parchment-covered dowel inside the bead, roll the clay-covered core over the texture block to make the impression. Make 2 of these red textured tube beads and bake according to the manufacturer's recommended temperature for 30 minutes.

6 When cool, sand each core lightly. Rub with gold acrylic paint and wipe off the excess with a soft cloth to reveal the texture block impression.

3

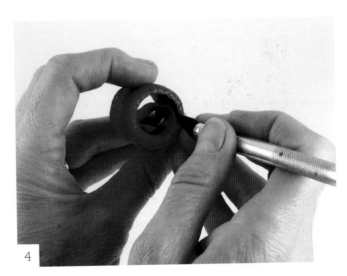

4

5

6

7 To make the 2 black, white, and gold tube beads, lightly coat two 3⁄8-inch (10mm) cores with liquid polymer.

8 Run a strip of black clay through on a pasta machine's thin setting (1 playing card)—this is a decorative element. Cut 2 strips that are 3⁄16 inch (5mm) wide. Wrap the strips around the middle of the cores. Trim and smooth the join.

9 Smooth the gold leaf on a 3-inch (8cm) square of gold clay that's been rolled on the pasta machine's thick setting (7–8 playing cards). Run the leaf-covered clay square through the pasta machine again at a medium setting (3–4 playing cards) to crackle the gold leaf.

10 Cut 4 strips of the crackled gold leaf 1⁄3 inch (8mm) wide. Place these thin gold strips on either side of the black strips.

11 Trim the gold leaf, and then use a texturizing tool such as coarse sandpaper or a pumice to add texture, adhere the gold leaf in place, and cover any irregularities.

7

8

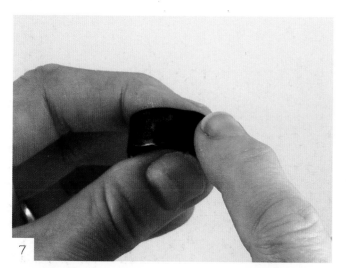

9

10

12 Cut thin slices from the white log and arrange the circles evenly on top of the central black strip.

13 To make the petals for the wider cane-covered "Buddha Bloom" beads, create 4 Skinner blends (see page 16) approximately 2⅜ × 2⅜ inches (6 × 6cm). Blend the pink chili, persimmon, ultra blue, and sea green clays with white as shown. Shape your persimmon/white Skinner blend into an elongated semicircle. With the dark pink at the base, wrap the sea green Skinner blend around it as shown in the photo. Repeat this process using the pink chili blend in the center

with the ultra blue blend on the outside. Reserve a little of your pink chili blend to make a tiny petal to nestle between the larger petals.

14 Reduce both canes to approximately ⅜ inch (10mm) high and ¼ inch (6mm) wide. Try to maintain the lotus petal shape as you reduce each cane. Depending on your penchant for bling, you can rub the outside of both canes with some gold Pearl Ex powder at this point. Don't Pearl-Ex the tiny petal cane—that would be going overboard.

11

12

13

14

15 To assemble the Buddha Bloom beads, smear a very thin layer of liquid polymer over each 1³/₁₆-inch (3cm) core and cover with a layer of red chili clay run through the pasta machine at a medium-thin setting (1–2 playing cards). Apply texture with your texturing tools.

16 Place 1 black and 2 crackled gold strips in the center of the 1³/₁₆-inch (3cm) tube just as you did for the accent beads (see steps 8–10). With a tissue blade, cut approximately 24 thin slices of your petal canes, 12 of each color. These should be approximately ¹/₁₆ inch (1mm) thick. Lightly press the petals on each side of the black and gold central strip, alternating the petal colors as you go around the bead. When you're happy with the placement, press them more firmly to adhere.

17 Use a needle tool to create a small indent in the base of the petals. Cut slices of the reserved pink chili blend to make a tiny pink petal. Place a small pink slice between each larger petal. Use a knitting needle to place and adhere the petal.

18 Finally add slices of your rested white roll. In the temples in Nepal, artists place these white dots at the base of the petals. Bake the beads according to the manufacturer's recommended temperature for 15 minutes.

15

16

17

18

19 String these lovely tube beads on the cording of your choice. If you are using a Nepali-style arrangement with multiple strands of seed beads, you may want to create polymer findings in order to gather the bead strands into cones at each end. Make each cone from a ball of black polymer approximately 3/8 inch (10mm) in diameter. Hollow the balls and make cone shapes. Decorate with a narrow strip of the crackled gold around the base, texture, and add white spots. Make a hole at the top to accommodate an eye pin.

20 To make a clasp, roll black clay on a medium-thick setting (5-6 playing cards). Cut a circle 3/4 inch (2cm) in diameter. In the center of this circle, cut out a 1/2-inch (13mm) circle. Wrap a thin strip of gold leaf polymer around the edge of the circle and then decorate with white spots. Texture lightly and then bake. You'll need to make a small hole in the rim of the circle to allow the clasp to be attached to the necklace with a jump ring.

Make a toggle that is approximately 1 3/8 inches (3.5cm) long and 3/16 inch (5mm) wide at its widest point. Put a hole in the toggle and bake. Thread the end of the strand of beads through the hole to attach it to the necklace.

19

20

"Seeing a unique shape or unusual color combination can be enough to get me started on a clay project." —REBECCA WATKINS

Rebecca Watkins

The Practical, Impatient Artist ➤ Pennsylvania, United States

Rebecca Watkins considers herself a methodical person, so it comes as a surprise to learn about her very loose and free-form approach to beadwork, combining an appreciation for texture and spontaneity into her signature style. She considers each bead a small canvas, applying abstract bits of color to the surface. Using those areas of color as her guide, she begins scratching and scribing to uncover an image or a design that she senses is hidden there. She adds paint or powder to further enhance the lines.

Over the years, Rebecca has tried almost every art and craft medium, including cross-stitch, crochet, rug hooking, mosaics, oil paint, pastels, flameworking, and enameling. She is especially drawn to mediums that provide immediate gratification, are relatively inexpensive, and don't require a dedicated space. Discovering polymer clay was a turning point, even though it took her multiple attempts. Her first experiments with polymer were crude disasters, and she gave up. Then in 2007, she thumbed through Judy Belcher's *Polymer Clay Creative Traditions* at a bookstore, and the projects prompted her to try again. Rebecca has doodled her way through many meetings as a corporate world graphic designer and writer, so when she saw that she could "draw" on clay, she was captivated. "To say I was obsessed for the first few years is an understatement. Even now, when I sit down at my work table I rarely have a specific end result in mind. Usually it's just a loose idea of colors or shape or a technique I want to try."

Rebecca is refreshingly clear about doing exactly what works and what pleases her. Through her online shop she has tapped into a worldwide audience of makers and carved out a niche that would have been impossible on a local scale. After selling polymer jewelry at a few shows, she soon discovered that these venues didn't provide a good return on her investment. "Finding time to build up inventory was difficult, and then I might sit at a show all day and barely make enough to cover the table cost," she recalls. "Worse yet, at least a third of all vendors at the shows were also jewelry makers. But that realization gave me an idea."

Clearly, there were many creative people who like to put beads together. So why not become their supplier? "I never liked having to guess what necklace lengths, metals, and findings would be popular. So instead, why not shift my focus to the part that I enjoyed?" she reasoned. Her biggest challenge was how to reach all those jewelry makers. Shortly after her bead epiphany, she learned about Etsy and opened a shop that enabled her to sell twenty-four hours a day. Instead of sitting in a booth for a whole day, hoping that a few attendees from a limited geographic region liked her wares, she could reach customers around the world while she worked and slept.

More often than not, Rebecca's immediate environment inspires her. "Interesting sunlight and shadows will prompt me to shoot a photo to use as reference for a drawing. Seeing a unique shape or unusual color combination can be

---

Opposite, clockwise from top left:

Rebecca Watkins in her studio, otherwise known as her dining room.

OomPahPah Pairs; ultralight clay, polymer, and metallic powder; each bead 1 inch (2.5cm).

Unravelled Beads; polymer; 1 inch (2.5cm). Using a long metal bolt, Rebecca textured a flat sheet of clay and randomly added bits of textured polymer to a base bead.

Fish in Turtleneck; polymer, 1 inch (2.5cm). One of many nattily dressed fish in this series.

enough to get me started on a clay project. I often daydream on my commute: 'What have I never seen before?' or 'What would the result be if I folded the clay like this and cut through it like that?'" She finds more visual creative stimulation through her local guild and online. "I love looking at everyone's work. Thinking about all the insanely talented people in the world would be depressing if it weren't so inspirational. I get the itch to try new mediums or get back to old ones when I see work I like." Once inspiration strikes, it's not unusual for her to stay up all night engrossed in a polymer project. The first time it happened, she didn't notice the passing hours until she was startled out of her quiet art reverie by chirping birds and the brightening sky at dawn. Her small home in Pittsburgh doesn't offer enough space for a dedicated studio, so her dining room table is often strewn with tools, bits of clay, a pasta machine, and remnants of other crafts that have caught her fancy. When visitors come, she contains the chaos in two giant cabinets in the living room. Rebecca explains, "People always ask if I have a studio. And I say, if by 'studio' you mean a table, then yes."

Despite her childhood dreams of becoming an artist and her breadth of experience, she didn't start feeling like an artist until just a few years ago. "I think it's very common for people who create to feel like they're not a 'real' artist unless they make a full-time living from their art or embed deep, mysterious meaning in their creations." Now, Rebecca allows inspiration and feedback from polymer clay enthusiasts around the world to carry her along. "Nonartists always ask, 'How do you know it will work out?' And I say, 'I don't, but figuring it out is the fun of it.' And maybe that's partially what makes one an artist: a lack of fear even though you don't quite know what you're doing. Now I have repeat customers, people comment favorably on items I post to Flickr, and other polymer artists want me to share my techniques. If that was happening to someone else, I'd call them an artist, so now I think the label fits me, too."

May Circus Beads; polymer and metallic powder; 1 inch (2.5cm). The circus changes colors with the season.

Scribed Bead; polymer; 2 inches (5cm). Rebecca often senses a pattern in the bead and cuts lines with a sharp stylus to enhance the design. The bead is then rolled in dark powder, baked, and sanded to reveal the lines.

Petal Circus Beads; polymer and metallic powders; 1 inch (2.5cm). Sometimes Rebecca leaves the overlays on the surface. Other times, she blends them into the bead.

Project:
Floral Scribed Beads By Rebecca Watkins

Rebecca is comfortable riding her wave of intuition. She imagines a scene on a bead and then brings her small canvas to life. For those of us who don't work as intuitively, she developed this tutorial for floral "scribed" beads. She suggests roughly applying pastel colors and then enhancing the resulting patterns with lines and powders. The step in which you cover your beads with black powder will make you think that you've made truly ugly beads. But hang on: The big reveal is quite remarkable! Rebecca's foolproof method encourages imperfections and invites you to add your own variations.

TOOLS AND MATERIALS

polymer clay in 5 or 6 complementary
    colors, plus scrap clay
smooth work surface
tissue blade
small awl or needle tool,
    approximately ¹/₁₆ inch (1mm)
    or ³/₃₂ inch (2mm) in diameter
small, fluffy paintbrush
Pearl Ex powder in carbon black
Perfect Pearls powder in gold
bead baking rack or flame-retardant
    polyester batting
sandpaper, 400-grit (3M Sandblaster
    Sheets)
automotive wet/dry sandpaper,
    1000-grit
soft cloth or piece of denim
    for polishing

> **TIP**
> I use Kato clay and bake my beads for
> 15 minutes at 278° F (137° C) to make
> them very sturdy. I can even throw them
> down hard on a tile floor and they bounce
> up unharmed. Kato clay holds its shape
> as I scribe the marks into a bead, and
> its hardness means that the final piece
> polishes to a nice shine with minimal effort.

INSTRUCTIONS

 Condition and roll 4 or 5 small sheets of clay on the pasta machine at the medium-thin setting (1-2 playing cards). Create a 5 × 5-inch (12.5 × 12.5cm) sheet for the background, plus 3 or 4 smaller squares in different colors for the flowers. Minor color variation and variegation help to create appealing visual movement. In the sample, the green is mottled, and there is some orange in the red square.

 Roll out a thick 5 × 8-inch (12.5 × 20.5cm) sheet of scrap clay (9-10 playing cards). Continue rolling on successively thinner levels until the sheet is 5 inches (12.5cm) wide and 12 inches (30.5cm) long (about 5 playing cards). Loosely fold it in half to a 5 × 6-inch

(12.5 × 15cm) sheet. Start at the folded end and roll the two layers into a log. (Donna Kato taught my guild this method, which makes a log with a perfectly spiraled center.)

 Wrap the log with a thin (1-2 playing cards) 5-inch (12.5cm) strip of your background color. The long edges of the wrap should meet but not overlap. Smooth the seam with your fingers.

4 Slice the log into 5 equal pieces with a tissue blade. Gradually pinch the cut ends of each bead-sized piece together to cover the scrap clay core color. Round the edges, moving to a barrel shape. Roll the barrel shape

1

2

3

4

into a sphere by applying even pressure between flat palms. The photo shows how the shape of each bead will progress from log to sphere.

5 Create a hole from end to end, following the path of the core center. When the point of the needle just begins to come out the other side, pull the needle out of the first side and enter it from the opposite end. This will ensure that both ends of the hole are smoothed inward to look uniform and well finished.

6 Tear small pieces of your first colors into triangle shapes; don't try to make them perfect.

7 Arrange 3 to 5 triangular pieces of the same color with points positioned inward to create a flower shape. Don't butt them up against each other; leave a little space.

Repeat with the remaining colors. Don't worry about spacing them perfectly; just observe as you place each one to ensure they are arranged in a way so that the flowers are visible from every angle. You can also add a single triangle near the edge of some flowers to represent a leaf.

8 Make tiny balls from a contrasting color. Squish them a bit and place 1 in the center of each flower.

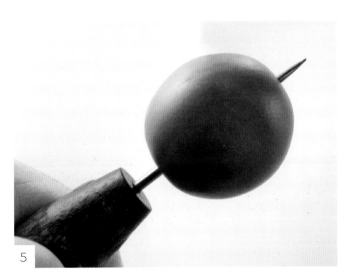

5

6

7

8

9 Roll each bead to press the flowers into the base. You can roll them all the way smooth or leave them slightly raised.

10 Holding the bead gently, use the needle tool to roughly outline the flower shapes. (Cynthia Tinapple dubbed this technique "scribing" so now that's what I call it too!) Add lines at the petal edges, outline the leaves, and add dots or a spiral in the center of each flower. Don't try to be perfect; it's better to freehand and go outside the lines. Lightly reroll the bead into a sphere if scribing has pushed it out of shape.

11 Redefine the hole in each bead again from each side. Brush the entire bead with a mix of carbon black Pearl Ex with a pinch of gold Perfect Pearls mixed in. Bake on a bead rack or batting according to the manufacturer's instructions for your clay.

9

10

TIP

I keep my mix in a little plastic tub, about 5 inches (12.5cm) across and about 4 inches (10cm) deep. I put about a tablespoon of black powder in the tub and add a quick shake of the gold to it, just enough to give it some shimmer. Too much gold "grays" down the black and then it's not dark enough (in my opinion). I usually place the bead on a skewer and hold it down in the tub to brush the powder on so it doesn't go airborne. If I'm making a lot of beads, I wear a mask for safety.

11

12   When the beads have cooled, sand the Pearl Ex off so that it remains only in the scribed lines. To remove the majority of the Pearl Ex, I like to use 400-grit 3M Sandblaster sheets which are flexible, purple-foam sheets that are perfect for round surfaces.

13   Finally, sand with 1000-grit wet/dry automotive sandpaper and buff. I buff by hand with jersey knit fabric or denim (often the clothes I'm wearing at the moment), or a soft cotton pillowcase. They all do a nice job. A bit of buffing leaves the beads glowing and ready for stringing.

12

13

New Zealand's Polymer

If you are living or traveling across the world, you may notice that each region has its own brands of polymer. Companies continue to develop new and exciting clays in a rainbow of colors with unique properties and increased durability. New on the scene, Du-kit brand is one such example of innovation through globalization. Founded and primarily used in New Zealand, Du-kit polymer clay is now becoming increasingly available in other countries and has inspired its own branded line of tools.

CHAPTER 8

Canes 2.0

Most polymer hobbyists begin by learning to build geometric canes but are soon lured to other processes and products. Those who stick with caning have discovered how to make polymer perform new tricks. Kim Korringa has developed clever ways of working and reworking polymer to create complex designs that nevertheless are perfect for production at a large scale. Kim and the caners in this chapter's gallery know their way around a cane, and they raise the question of how to apply new approaches to tried-and-true techniques.

Opposite, clockwise from top left:

Sabine Spiesser, *Gift for an African Queen*; polymer, horn, bronze clay, and metal; 21 inches (53cm). Photograph by the artist. This Australian artist's design was inspired by memories from growing up in Angola, Africa.

Ellen Prophater, *Earring Dishes*; polymer, embossing powder, glass beads, and silver findings. Ellen manages and co-owns a gallery at the Creative Journeys Studio in Buford, Georgia.

Cornelia Brockstedt, *Coastline Necklace*; polymer; 21 inches (53cm). Cornelia runs a small graphic design studio in northern Germany and creates polymer and silver jewelry in her spare time. No matter which media she is working in, she is inspired by the Bauhaus concept "form follows function."

Mira Pinki Krispil, *Zentangle on Polymer Vase*; polymer, markers, and glass; 7 x 3 inches (18 x 7.5cm). This Israeli artist discovered the joys of working with polymer during physical therapy following an operation on her hands.

Meisha Barbee, *Shimmer Pendant*, 2011; polymer with sterling silver. The silver loop embedded in the clay becomes integral to Meisha's design. Her studio is located in the Spanish Village Art Center in San Diego, California.

Silvia Ortiz de la Torre, *Spring Rose Windows Necklace*; polymer and silver; 31 inches (79cm). The canework by this Spanish artist reflects her fascination for finding patterns in everything from soap film to fractals.

Carol Simmons, *Covered Eggs*; polymer on egg shells; 2¼ inches tall (5.7cm). Carol has developed a technique that allows her to apply her signature kaleidoscope cane design over eggs.

Jan Montarsi, *Aztec Pendant*; mica polymer; 3 inch diameter (7.5cm). Jan uses a technique known as *mica mush*, which takes advantage of the luster in metallic polymer to produce blended clays in glowing colors.

Alice Stroppel, *Sweater Girl Pendant*; polymer; 1 inch tall (2.5cm). Alice used her signature scrap cane technique to create the sweater for this piece. Her process is one example of a polymer revolution that spread thanks to online communities and sharing.

Julie Eakes, *DaVinci Pendant*; polymer and rubber cord; 3 x 3 inches (7.5 x 7.5cm). A thin slice of Julie's polymer mosaic portrait is framed in a shadow box frame that is encrusted with designs. Inspired by Italian architecture, Julie surrounds her mosaics with many layers and ornate shapes.

Dusdee Chotipruk, *Joyful Mobile*; fiber, polymer, glass beads, wire, and brass findings; 28 inches (71cm). This well-traveled Thai artist's masterful canework represents the new modern tribal aesthetic.

Angela Barenholtz, *Pendant 903*; polymer with silver bail; 3 inches long (7.5cm). Israeli artist Angela uses a variation of a technique that she's developed for creating tweeds and woven fabric-like canes. She freely shared this technique online.

Debbie Jackson, *Wanna Trade?*; polymer clay, African brass, dyed horn, ostrich shell disks, and recycled glass beads; each 20–30 inches (50–76.2cm). Photograph by the artist. Using polymer canes, Debbie imitates old trade beads, which were exchanged for gold, oil, ivory, and slaves.

Megan Newberg, *Snowflake Ornament*; polymer over glass; 3 inches (7.5cm). Tucscon-based artist Megan likes the challenge of figuring out easy ways to make complex canes, often inspired by quilt patterns and complex patterns from other textiles.

Dede Leupold, *Tropical Tantrum Earrings*; polymer and sterling silver; 2 inches long (5cm). Photograph by the artist. In this cane, Dede tried to include more colors and veer away from symmetry. You can compare these photos to see how the cane (left) was reduced for the earrings.

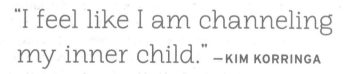

"I feel like I am channeling my inner child." —KIM KORRINGA

Kim Korringa
Chaos and Control ➤ California, United States

For many years, Kim Korringa resisted calling herself an artist because it seemed pretentious. "Art is a passion, a need, a compulsion. I feel like I am channeling my inner child, and I have to surround myself with things of my own making. Others may want to own or buy an object they admire, but I want to experience the process of giving birth to it," she says. Kim has been making and selling polymer for more than twenty years, but her approach still feels fresh. Her aesthetic gravitates to rich, saturated colors, with an abundance of detail, pattern, and voluptuous forms. In Kim's world, more is more. She is attracted to anything with concentric circles, which she finds on clothing, household furnishings, and knickknacks. Even her doodles are full of circles. While Kim has no idea why she developed this fascination, it explains her attraction to millefiori canework, beginning with the graphic and colorful canes made by Martha Breen in the early 1990s.

Growing up, Kim's ability to distract and entertain herself by creating things was her refuge in a childhood home that became increasingly chaotic and dysfunctional. She admits that "to this day when I am creating, I am in the zone where my thoughts drift off, time is irrelevant, and I am content." Her love of jewelry and personal adornment began when she was a young child; as she recalls, "A family friend we were visiting put a rubber band on my wrist. She tucked little flowers under it, making a living bracelet for me." Before she was old enough for pierced ears, she drew tiny paper flowers that she glued to her earlobes. "I licked the tips of the colored pencils so that the color would be ultrasaturated. No wimpy pastel colors for me!" she says. This color palette has appealed to her ever since.

Plants and flowers around her childhood home in Sonoma County contributed to her lifelong love affair with complex designs found in nature. "I would take one of my mother's oil-painting brushes and pretend to be painting the color on the flowers. I roamed freely in our yard, peeling bark off tree trunks, popping fuchsia buds, smearing calla lily pollen on my skin, licking the nectar from honeysuckle blossoms," she says. She sold seeds she'd collected from plants, packaging them in envelopes with her drawings of the flowers on the front, to her neighbors. She pressed and dried flowers, or strung them with a needle and thread to make leis. Kim even painted her bedroom walls in flowering vines that mingled with actual Algerian ivy vines that were growing on the wall, creeping in through a missing window louver.

In the early 1980s, when technology was booming, Kim moved to the heart of Silicon Valley. Computers had not yet replaced the human hand, so she lucked into architectural drafting and technical illustrating jobs that required steady hands and a patient, precise nature. Although she was successful at work, her personal art suffered from the preciseness she brought home from the job. "I would fuss, using tiny brushes and a straightedge ruler. My art

Opposite, clockwise from top left:

Kim Korringa surrounded by her work in her California studio.

Pressed Flowers Brooch; polymer; 2 x 3 inches (5 x 7.5cm).

Vessel; polymer; 5 inches (12.5cm). The clay was cut using a technique developed by Carol Zilliacus.

Mosaic Pin; polymer; 2 inches wide (5cm). Kim was inspired to create this pin after a workshop with Cynthia Toops at the Arrowmont School of Arts and Crafts.

Fantasy Flower Necklace; polymer with glass, stone, and brass beads; 24 inches (61cm).

lacked the spontaneity and joy that I wanted to express," she says.

Kim found the right balance between chaos and control in caning when she discovered polymer clay in 1992. "The beautiful part about caning was that while you could be precise and plan all you wanted, the final product would invariably have a wonky, slightly imperfect look to it, especially in my earliest canes. I liked that I could control it only so much. Then I had to accept what I got," Kim says. Over the years she learned to correct for distortion and plan her canes, but she still lives for that magical moment when she slices into a cane to see what's inside.

While Kim's art is in high demand, she most values her personal connection with the people who wear her jewelry. "I know I could charge more for my work, but part of the thrill for me is making my art accessible. I think of my own pocketbook when I set my prices and I want ordinary people to be able to enjoy my work. It means I can make more!" Kim admits. This commitment keeps her busy. She sells her pieces at eight to ten shows each year; Kim even worked twelve- to fifteen-hour workdays for months at a stretch to fulfill a catalog's order for 1,100 Christmas items.

Kim says that she used to envy artists who could ascribe deep meaning to their artwork. "I felt that I was missing out, that I didn't take my work seriously enough. Now I freely admit that I do what I love and what makes me happy," she says. Kim can still remember how her mother painted in oils, and when Kim smelled turpentine in the house she would know that her mother was in her "happy place." Kim hopes that "maybe, years from now when my grown kids smell polymer clay curing in an oven, they will be transported back to days when their mama was happily claying."

Tropical Fairy Wings

When women from Samunnat (see page 125) were shown the works of American artists, they immediately picked up Kim's earrings with beaming smiles and obvious excitement. Kim's colors and designs were a perfect fit for these young women a world away. With Kim's blessing they learned how to incorporate her methods into their work. Her color palette resonated with their tropical surroundings and the graceful petal shapes looked right at home in Nepal.

Project:
Fairy Wing Earrings By Kim Korringa

These dainty little fairy wing earrings were inspired by fuchsia flowers in Kim's garden. She originally made them in combinations of pink, purple, and red to look like the flowers, but they evolved into every imaginable color combination. The canes she uses for the petals are simple and graphic, their patterns playing against the curvy, organic shape of the flower. Kim's secret for making these beads is a baking form that she developed from scrap clay, allowing the petals to preserve their shape as the clay bakes. In this project, you'll learn how to make the baking form and pick up several quick and easy techniques for recombining canes.

Kim makes her flowers into earrings with tiny pearls hanging from their centers, but they could also be strung together like a lei or grouped into bouquet arrangements for pins or pendants. Once you learn the technique, your garden of creative ideas will bloom.

TOOLS AND MATERIALS

polymer clay: solid-color scraps
    plus 3 graduated canes or
    Skinner-blend canes (see page 16)

2 quilter's T-pins

U.S. size 8 (5mm) knitting needle
    or pencil

smooth work surface

cornstarch or talcum powder

metallic Mylar film (Jones Tones;
    optional)

deli wrap or waxed paper

bone folder or spoon, for burnishing

brayer or acrylic rod

tissue blade

Kato Repel Gel (optional)

head pin and earring findings

INSTRUCTIONS

1. The baking form that I created is made from a quilter's T-pin and some scrap clay. Roll the scrap clay into 2 equal olive-size balls. Pierce each clay ball directly through the center with a pin and bury the T end in the clay with the point protruding out the other side. Flatten the bottom T end of the clay and shape the tops of each ball of clay until they are symmetrically arched domes. Bake these forms according to the manufacturer's instructions for 30 minutes.

2. For the bull's-eye petal cane you will need 3 blends in contrasting colors rolled into basic canes. Instead of creating Skinner blends, I wrap 4 or 5 individual layers of increasingly lighter or darker clay. This more time-consuming method yields a very large gradated cane that I can use for many projects. You may choose to use my preferred method or create your canes using Skinner blends.

3. Using my knitting needle technique, you can quickly turn basic graduated canes into many cane combinations as shown in the photo. Use a knitting needle (or a pencil) to pierce a hole all the way through the center of one of your basic graduated blend canes. Roll the cane on its side as if it were a wheel on an axle. Roll it until the hole in the center enlarges to about half the diameter of the cane.

4. Reduce one of the remaining basic canes until it's slightly smaller than the hole you've opened up in the first cane. Dust the smaller cane with cornstarch or talcum. Wiggle the smaller cane into the hole in the

1

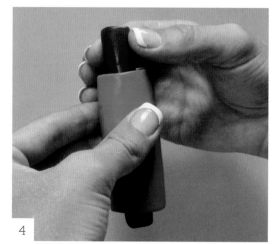

2

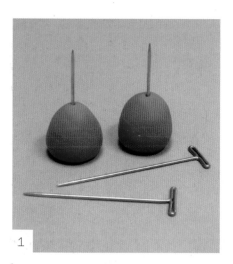

3

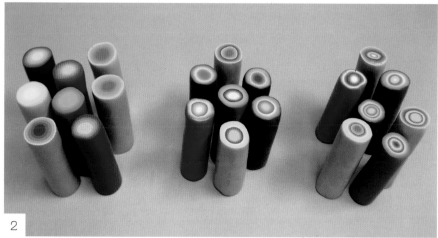

4

center of the first cane. Squeeze the 2 canes together by pressing gently, starting at the center of the log and moving toward the ends to avoid trapping air.

5   To make a triple bull's-eye cane, simply repeat the knitting needle technique with a third gradated blend cane. You'll need to reduce the double bull's-eye cane in diameter in order to fit it into the third cane. You will have leftover double bull's-eye cane to use for a different cane. You can see how your options for combinations are expanding.

6   To add a subtle touch of bling to the petals, you may wrap the outside of a finished cane in a layer of clay that has had Jones Tones metallic Mylar film applied to it. Roll out a thin sheet of clay large enough to wrap around your cane. Lay the sheet flat on deli wrap or waxed paper and burnish the Jones Tones onto the surface thoroughly with a bone folder, the back of a spoon, or other burnishing tool. Rip the backing off to leave the metallic finish on the clay. You can burnish Jones Tones onto any missed spots again. Wrap this sheet around your cane with the metallic surface on the outside of the cane. Check for bubbles, slicing through the clay to release any trapped air. The added bonus of Jones Tones is that raw canes finished this way will not stick together when you store them.

7   Reduce your triple bull's-eye cane to about ¾ inch (2cm) in diameter. With a brayer or rod, roll and flatten the cane into a long, thin oval. When the pattern is twice as wide as it is tall, slice the cane in half lengthwise.

Shape these two halves into petals by pinching the cut edges together and trimming off the excess ragged clay. You can perfect the shape and size of the petals by stroking and pulling on the cane until the petals are about the size of a small fingernail. Let the cane rest before you slice it. I firm up my canes by laying them on paper to leach out some plasticizer (see page 15). A firmer cane is easier to slice and shape. Sometimes I even put a soft cane in the freezer for 5 minutes to firm up before slicing.

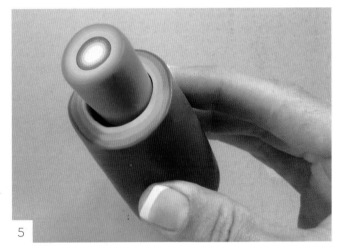

5

6

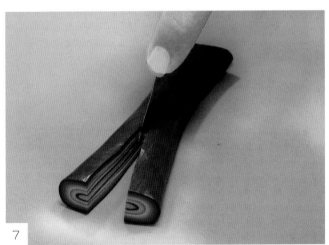

7

8 Cut 4 slices of these petal canes about the thickness of a dime or 1/16 inch (1.4mm). After each slice, flip the cane onto a different side so you don't keep distorting the cane in the same direction. Arrange these 4 slices on your work surface in a cross configuration. In the center of the cross put a small ball of scrap clay that overlaps the petals slightly. This assures that all the petals are attached to each other when you transfer them to the baking form. Press all parts of the flower against your work surface with your fingertip.

9 Slide your tissue blade under the petal group to remove the flower from your work surface. Pierce the center of the flower with the T-pin baking form and let the petals drape over the form very gently without distorting the shape. Smooth the flower very lightly, but don't burnish it onto the form or it will be difficult to remove it after baking! Make another 4-petal flower to layer over the first flower, alternating the position of the petals. Smooth the top layer of petals very gently over the bottom layer. You can use the same cane for the second layer of petals, but it is more interesting to use a different cane that has contrasting colors and patterns. Bake the flowers on their forms for 30-40 minutes.

Remove the flowers from the forms while they are still hot. They tend to stick if they cool. I like to remove the hot flowers from the forms under running water so that after they come off, they immediately firm up and set their shape in the cold water. Alternatively, before you start assembling you can coat the baking forms with Repel Gel to keep the baked petals from sticking.

For an earring, you may dangle small beads from the center of the flower on a wire. Form the top of the wire into a loop and attach it to an earring finding. You may prefer to gather a few flowers into a brooch bouquet or string them together as beads.

8

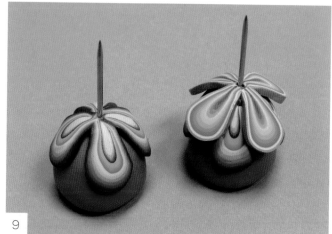

9

Polymer Masters

It may be impolite, but I think of the artists in this gallery as "sneezers"—that is, evangelists for our craft. They travel, teaching and spreading the germs of their techniques all over the world. When one of these teachers hosts a class, variations of his or her style soon appear in online galleries as students practice what they've learned and the polymer "bug" takes hold. Sneezers' ideas and styles are contagious. Thanks to these artists and others like them, polymer has gone viral.

Christi Friesen, *Paradise Revisited Vessel*; polymer, glass form, pearls, stones, and acrylic paint; 10 x 6 x 4 inches (25.5 x 15 x 10cm). Photograph by the artist. Christi travels throughout the U.S. and internationally teaching techniques to achieve her instantly recognizable look.

Louise Fischer-Cozzi, *Wholey Necklace/Belt*; silver findings. When this Brooklyn-based artist is not teaching American and European guilds, she may be found at her summer home in Stresa, Italy, on Lago Maggiore.

Carol Simmons, *Korean Embroidery Cane Lentil Beads*; polymer; each 2 inch diameter (5cm). Carol cites her work mapping vegetation in California, the Rocky Mountains, and the Arctic as inspiration for her work. Korean embroidery provided the color palette for this cane.

Ronna Sarvas Weltman, *Natural Selection Necklace*; polymer, fine silver, sterling silver, and black wax; 34-inch (86-cm) strand. Photograph by Doug Yaple. Ronna teaches at polymer artist retreats as well as on craft cruises.

Melanie West, *The Maw Bracelet*; polymer. Photograph by the artist. This organic bracelet is just one of the New England artist's series of Biobangles. Created in her studio in the woodlands of Maine, Melanie's work has been shown in exhibits everywhere, from Japan to Spain and Switzerland to Canada.

Judy Belcher, *Micro Knitting Cuffs*; polymer over copper; ¼ to 2 inches in width (6mm to 5cm). Photograph by the artist. Judy's love of Italian Missoni knitwear—and lack of knitting ability— led her to create this technique.

Sarah Shriver, *Frida Flower Bracelet*; polymer; each 2 inches long (5cm). Photograph by George Post. Sarah first discovered polymer in 1987 and, early on, was influenced by the work of Judith Skinner and Martha Breen.

Kathleen Halverson Dustin, *Blumen Bachia Purse*; polymer with rubber handle; 9 x 4½ x 4½ inches (23 x 11 x 11cm). Kathleen's purses are displayed in several museums, including the permanent collection of the Tassenmuseum (Museum of Bags and Purses) in Amsterdam. A polymer pioneer, Kathleen continues to teach around the world.

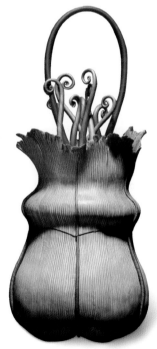

Lisa Pavelka, *Blue Spinner Ring*; polymer and metal finding; 1 inch (2.5cm). The top of this ring can twist off when the wearer wants a change. A Colorado native now residing in Las Vegas, Lisa teaches and develops new products for the polymer market.

Jana Roberts Benzon, *Luscious*; polymer, metal, and freshwater pearl; 2 x 4 inches (5 x 10cm). Photograph by the artist. An international teacher, Jana draws inspiration from old-world decorative motifs.

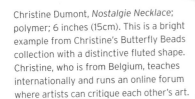

Christine Dumont, *Nostalgie Necklace*; polymer; 6 inches (15cm). This is a bright example from Christine's Butterfly Beads collection with a distinctive fluted shape. Christine, who is from Belgium, teaches internationally and runs an online forum where artists can critique each other's art.

Bettina Welker, *Sphere Bracelet*; 2¾ x 3½ inches (7 x 9cm). Photograph by the artist. Bracelets are one of Bettina's favorite forms, and the subject of her book, *Polymer Clay Bracelets*, which was published simultaneously in German and English.

Sandra McCaw, *Floating Leaves Neckpiece, Spring*; polymer, gold-filled wire, glass beads, diamonds, and 23K gold leaf; 18 x 3 inches (45.5 x 7.5cm). Photograph by Hap Sakwa. Sandra has taught extensively throughout Europe and is known for her distinctive McCaw Cane.

Donna Kato, *Split Pod Neckpiece*; polymer and rubber cord; 5 inches long (12.5cm). Donna is famous for her tapering forms and zipper canes, which are central to this contemporary organic design.

Lisa Pavelka, *Textile Effect Bangle*; polymer and wood; 4 x 4 x ½ inches (10cm x 10cm x 13mm). Created as part of Lisa's *Geo Bangle* series, this piece includes caning and surface techniques on polymer that is wrapped over a wooden armature.

Dayle Doroshow, *Flower Burst 1 Brooch*; polymer; 4 x 4½ inches (10 x 11.5cm). Photograph by the artist.

Tory Hughes, *Kilauea Brooch*; polymer, acrylic, and gold; 2 x 1½ inches (5 x 3.8cm). From Tory's Aquarelle Collection, this brooch is named after a volcano on the north shore of Kauai, Hawaii.

Lindly Haunani, *Folded Petal Brooch*; translucent polymer over a sterling silver armature; 3 x 1 inches (7.5 x 2.5cm). Photograph by Hap Sakwa. Influenced by her Hawaiian heritage, Lindly designed this brooch as part of a series depicting the overlap of just budding tropical flowers.

Resources

The major manufacturers of clay and supplies are listed here but this is by no means a comprehensive list. New manufacturers and brands are appearing as demand increases for polymer and related supplies around the globe.

For additional, up-to-date information for suppliers, manufacturers, and artists, visit this book's companion website at PolymerClayGlobal.com.

MANUFACTURERS

Polyform Products
19901 Estes Avenue
Elk Grove Village, IL 60007
847-427-0020
sculpey.com
Premo! Sculpey, Sculpey III,
Sculpey UltraLight, polymer tools

Staedtler
Staedtler Mars Limited
5725 McLaughlin Road
Mississauga, Ontario L5R3K5
fimo.com
Fimo Classic, Fimo Soft, polymer tools

Van Aken International
9157 Rochester Court
P.O. Box 1680
Rancho Cucamonga, CA 91729
katopolyclay.com
Kato Polyclay, polymer tools

Viva Décor
495 East Erie Avenue
Philadelphia, PA 19124
215-634-2235
viva-décor.us
Pardo Art Clay, Pardo Jewellery
Clay, paints

Ranger Industries, Inc.
15 Park Road
Tinton Falls, NJ 07724
732-389-3535
rangerink.com
Embossing powders, inks

SUPPLIERS

The Cutting Edge
dancormier.com/
cuttingedgestore.html
Precision cutting tools for
polymer clay

Fire Mountain Gems and Beads
One Fire Mountain Way
Grants Pass, OR 97526
800-423-2319
firemountaingems.com
Metalsmithing tools and supplies,
jewelry-making tools and supplies

Polymer Clay Express
9890 Main Street
Damascus, MD 20872
800-844-0138
polymerclayexpress.com
All brands of polymers, polymer tools

Prairie Craft Company
P.O. Box 209
Florissant, CO 80816
800-799-0615
prairiecraft.com
Kato Polyclay, Kato tools, videos

Rio Grande
7500 Bluewater Road, N.W.
Albuquerque, NM 87121
riogrande.com
Jewelry-making tools and supplies,
metalsmithing tools and supplies

FEATURED ARTISTS

Shay Aaron
Tel Aviv-Yafo, Israel
facebook.com/shayaaronminiatures

Fabiola Pérez Ajates
Madrid, Spain
fabicontusmanos.blogspot.com

Gera Scott Chandler
Victoria, BC, Canada
gerascottchandler.com

Christine Damm
Braintree, Vermont, USA
storiestheytell.blogspot.com

Tejae Floyde
Colorado Springs, Colorado, USA
tejaesart.com

Natalia García de Leániz
Madrid, Spain
tatanatic.com

Eva Haskova
Prague, Czech Republic
multidesign.cz

Kim Korringa
Mountain View, California, USA
kimcreates.com

Claire Maunsell
Gatineau, Quebec, Canada
stillpointworks.blogspot.com

Wendy Moore
Broken Hill, New South Wales,
Australia
afterthemonsoon.com

Cynthia Tinapple
Worthington, Ohio, USA
polymerclayglobal.com

Rebecca Watkins
Pittsburgh, Pennsylvania, USA
artybecca.blogspot.com

Genevieve Williamson
New Freedom, Pennsylvania, USA
genevievewilliamson.com

Camille Young
Tucson, Arizona, USA
camilleart.com

About the Author

Cynthia Tinapple ► Ohio, United States

Art and communications. I have spent my life bouncing between these two impulses, equally at home in the studio as I am in front of a word processor. My blog, *Polymer Clay Daily,* is just as much a work of art as the polymer pieces I have been creating since I first began to play with clay.

In the late 1980s, my daughter and I discovered polymer as we made food for her dollhouse. She outgrew the dollhouse, but I never outgrew polymer! When I saw early Ford and Forlano polymer jewelry in the Museum of Modern Art gift shop, a light went on in my brain. I signed up for classes, joined the new local guild, and got in on the ground floor of the national guild. Soon another local convert, Hollie Mion, and I were writing the national newsletter and attending as many events as we could manage. My husband is a cabinetmaker and wood turner with whom I have collaborated to create a space that reflects our artistic spirits. He has been willing to knock down walls and then saw, hammer, drill, grind, and sand his way through our home, where I have inlaid polymer into floors, stairways, sinks, switch plates, knobs, lamps, and bowls.

Capitalizing on my skills in communication, I found polymer friends online at CompuServe and Prodigy in the early days of the Internet. My experience working with public broadcasting and creating the first websites for a number of state agencies had convinced me of the importance of the Web. I built a family website. But as they grew older, my two children and stepson were not happy with being celebrated by their mother online. They were right. I agreed that I needed to shift my focus, and in 2005 I started my blog, *Polymer Clay Daily,* where writing a post each day became a habit.

I leaned on my friends for links at first. When I reached one thousand viewers a day, I figured I'd saturated the market. But then the Europeans started visiting. Artists working in related fields saw that they could mix polymer with their mediums. Social media kicked in, and the numbers continued to grow.

It's been a wild ride that has made me more disciplined and more active in retirement than I was when I worked. The stories from these makers and the heartfelt comments from thousands of others around the world make me both humble and grateful. As the community has grown, it has not lost its basic generosity and spirit.

Index

Note: page numbers in italics refer to picture captions.